With God, Grace, & Girlfriends

To Heathur Rose,
I hope you enjoy this book &
that it inspires you to connect more
deeply with the girlfriends in your
life!

May your journey be grace-filled,

With God Grace & Girlfriends

Lessons from Five Decades of Living

By Sheila Denise Townsend

With God, Grace & Girlfriends

By Sheila Denise Townsend

Copyright © **2018 Sheila Townsend**

ISBN-13: 978-1-7325930-0-8

Book cover design by Jamyla Townsend
Front cover background image by Sabina Salla

Printed by DiggyPOD in the United States of America

Disclaimer: The author has left out changed names and identifying details to protect the privacy of individuals. The author has tried to recreate events, locales and conversations from the author's memory of them. In order to maintain privacy, the author has in some instances left out the name and identifying details of individuals. Although the author has made every effort to make sure all information is correct at press time, the author does not assume and hereby disclaim any liability to any party for any loss, damage, disruptions caused by stories with this book, whether such information is a result of errors or emission, accident, slander or other cause.

Permission:
For information on getting permission for reprints and excerpts, contact: author.sdtownsend@gmail.com

Unless otherwise noted, Scripture quotations and references are taken from The Holy Bible, New King James Version® (NKJV). Copyright© 1982 by Thomas Nelson. Used by permission. All rights reserved.

www.sheiladtownsend.com

For Mommy.
Thank you.
Deuteronomy 6:5-9

For Daddy.
It's ok. Thank you.
John 15:13

For Jai.
You are so deeply loved.
Be happy, baby.
Be happy.
Romans 8:28-39

TABLE OF CONTENTS

ACKNOWLEDGMENTS

Michael Townsend, you have been everything I have needed you to be, in every season. Thank you for listening to me read between two and fifty sentences at any given moment. Thank you for always saying, "that's good, babe." Thank you for never letting me forget that I have something to say and for listening when no one else would. I love you.

Along this journey, I have had so much encouragement and support that it is difficult to name everyone.

To my listeners: Sandra Morrow, Yvette Fleetwood, Yvonne Clark, and my Vision 2021 Sisters. Thank you for your patience and kindness.

To my cheerleaders: Mary Grant and Amy Linkous. Because of your friendship, I am a better writer and person. Thank you.

To my Saturday morning prayer warriors. Thank you for the weekly reminder that I am a part of a long legacy of faith, laughter, and love.

To all of my girlfriends who traveled from far and wide to celebrate my fiftieth birthday and who will be the first readers of my published work. Your support is priceless. Thank you.

To my sisters: Nowadays, we laugh at how I fantasized about being an only child when we were young. Oh! How I wished you all away in my teenaged dreams—especially the twins. All these years later, I am so proud to be a part of Bobba Jean's girls! You all inspire me with your beauty, loyalty, and your love of Christ. I am not the easiest personality among us. Thank you for loving me anyway.

PROLOGUE

A shes to ashes; dust to dust. This is a commonly uttered phrase used to punctuate the end of a person's physical life. These six small words somehow manage to perfectly summarize the brevity, mystery, and simplicity of our journey on earth. Natural life is grand, beautiful, colorful, disorienting, and clamorous; but, in the end, it is merely the by-product of ashes and dust. Our bodies were spun to life from the dirt of the earth, the residue of her history and wisdom, and we are fated to return to her in the same state. Between these bookends—our natural beginning and our natural ending—we live. We rise and retreat, come and go, and gain and lose. We allow strangers to become friends and lose friends who were once like family. We discover great bubbles

13

of joy in unexpected places and are overwhelmed by heart-wrenching sorrow in the midst of contentment. We offend those we love most and forgive those who do not love us enough. We are ever learning who we are and are always transforming into who we are meant to be.

We are eternal, spiritual beings. However, although our physical journey is only a small fraction of eternity, it is important. In our natural state, we are introduced to our possibilities and are given the opportunities necessary for us to develop our whole being. We are set on a path from birth that is meant to carry us through a myriad of experiences where we are continuously transformed into ever-ascending versions of ourselves. Nevertheless, life gets in the way. We are waylaid on our journey by the burdens of living. Modern society compels us into a state where we get stuck in survival mode. We become like the children of Israel in the wilderness, navigating around the same mountain again and again. Yet, God has empowered us, through Christ, to turn in a different direction. If we are open and willing to trust Him, we change. We grow. We evolve. We become.

I recently read over old journal entries, and I was amazed by how much had not changed. The hot emotions that perpetually linger around me then still visit me now. The insecurities that constantly nipped at my heels many years ago have not gone away. The people and circumstances that filled me with gratitude as I wrote those entries are still present in my life. In contrast, I am also happy to note how much I have changed. Although old emotions still visit, they are never allowed to stay for very long. They have become a very short hallway that I must sometimes walk through instead of a dwelling place where I take up residence. I am no longer paralyzed by the bite of my insecurities. Experience has taught me that I am not alone. We all suffer from the fear that we do not measure up in some way. But we can refuse to allow our shortcomings to determine the height of our self-love and esteem. And, while I still find joy and comfort in the relationships that have endured, there are others that I have released because they did not edify, honor, or elevate me. Although my life may not be very far removed from where it was then, I am different. I am better. My world has not changed much, but I have.

As I celebrate my fiftieth year of life, I reflect on the many gifts and lessons I have gleaned, even as I acknowledge the brevity and impermanence of it all. It goes by so fast! But in each frame, there is layer upon layer of choices, words, thoughts, and deeds that create a beautiful mosaic of faith, grace, and friendship. I hope you learn to see the splendor and substance of your personal story as you read about mine.

CHAPTER 1

INTRODUCTION

*M*om, *life is hard.*

Three running dots bounced in sequence below my daughter's text message, indicating there was more to come. I stared at them in anticipation as I let her last statement push its way more deeply into my consciousness.

Life is hard.

It landed on top of my thoughts with a thud and began to wiggle and push, attempting to negotiate with my mind for agreement. I didn't want to agree with it—at least not as it stood, alone. I wanted a cushion, a *but* something. *But* anything. Yet, all I got was bouncing dots. So, I prepared myself to respond. I tried to conjure up my own *but* statement.

But, it gets better. That felt empty. Because sometimes it doesn't get better. Sometimes you just end up understanding yourself, your situation, and those around you differently.

But, it gets easier. That felt dishonest, because it doesn't really get easier. You get tougher. You get smarter. You get wiser. And what once felt impossible becomes manageable.

As I struggled to come up with a response that was both true and comforting, my heart squeezed in my chest. Not with hopelessness, but with a tinge of melancholy encased in a shell of iron certainty. I knew that this would be a heavy, defining moment for her. It is a moment we all encounter in one form or another. We enter that space where youth—fantastic dreams, unanchored imaginings, and unfailing belief in our supernatural abilities—comes to an end. Early in life, we start our journey toward fulfilling our dreams, full speed ahead, with an energy and a joie de vivre that can only be found in youth. One day, usually in our early adulthood, we hit a speed bump or pothole that slows our heedless, full run toward our fantastic vision. We then trot more carefully. Before long, our doubts and detractors draw more of our focus than our dreams, and the trot becomes a walk. The vision of the future that was once so clear becomes foggy, and our certainty about what was to come is lost in the noise of overwhelming, present struggles. The possibilities of life shrink from endless to a size that fits a more limited field of vision. Our perspective is changed in a monumental way as we learn the single lesson that seats us firmly in adulthood and heralds the final breath of childhood: life is hard.

Long before my daughter sent that text to me, I had spent many hours thinking, praying, and talking about the challenges she had faced in her life. Her journey into young adult independence was tumultuous for me. There was the joy of watching her graduate from undergrad and postgrad programs, mingled with the anxiety and sadness I felt because she was no longer at home. Next came the excitement of watching her make new friends and connections, giving her the community and support for which she'd hoped, mixed with the fear that these strangers may one day betray her. There was the tension of waiting for career possibilities to bear fruit, followed by the relief of her first job offer. Then, there was the crushing disappointment and rejection she felt when, less than a year later, she was fired from her first "real" job.

With each of her experiences, I held my breath. Even though I hoped for the best, I knew that disappointment and rejection were inevitable. Still, I prayed that it would be different for her. I prayed that God would instruct life to be kind to her. I wanted unusual, uncommon kindness to wrap around her and cocoon, cushion, and protect her from the sharp edges. I wanted God to recreate a space of comfort for her adult life that mirrored the space I had created for her as a child. There would always be food and shelter, she would have the financial resources she needed, true friendship would find her, and strangers would show her favor. But that is not life. Life is hard.

Most parents hope for an easy life for their children. It is not popular to say, and some of us may deny it. But, if given the opportunity to guarantee struggle-free days for our children, we wouldn't hesitate to take it. This desire motivates our endeavors from their childhood to shield them from the bumps and bruises that come with growing up—so much so that ensuring their safety and comfort often takes up prime real estate in our own lives. We constantly remind them that they are precious to us with words of affirmation. We are fierce in our defense of them and relentless in our hopes for them. We listen, we carry, we feed, we nurse, we entertain, we consider, we give, and we forgive. We love them with the very best of us, and we strive to be better so that we can love them more. We sacrifice our time, our money, our energy, and our desires all to ensure that they know they are well loved. Yet, even with all of our effort, we cannot shield our children from experiencing the hardships that come with living.

Watching our sons and daughters bump into and negotiate the inevitable, unavoidable moments that prune and shape them can be excruciating. We have to stand by as they encounter, in adolescence and adulthood, the difficulties from which we spent their whole childhood futilely laboring to protect them, while internally grappling with what this teaches us about our own journey and ourselves. We learn more about who our children are becoming. We support from the sidelines as they practice using the strength they have while building the strength they need. We squirm as we struggle not to jump in, often failing. Over time, we—hopefully—learn the lesson of the butterfly in the cocoon: the struggle of exiting the cocoon is necessary in order to build the wing strength a butterfly needs to survive. Assistance does not help the butterfly. In fact, protecting the budding creature from its struggle would only wound and sabotage its potential, sentencing the butterfly to a life without flight. If our children are to learn to fly, we have to accept the truth. They will struggle, and they will hurt. Life is hard.

The process of growing into a comfortable version of the independent self is beautiful. It's also tricky and exquisitely painful. The journey is filled with contradictory experiences that break us down in order to make us whole. It produces hurt that becomes the salve needed to heal. It is low points that bring great clarity and high points that birth our greatest disappointments. And, in the end, we struggle to forget it while holding the memories close all at the same time. Life's beauty and pain are inextricably connected. The seed of one holds the blossom of the other. Our greatest struggles in life come from our efforts to hoard the beauty while avoiding the pain.

I looked at my daughter's text message over and over again. The bouncing dots had long disappeared. She had nothing else to say. She had no words to bridge the gap between her reality and my heart, and I am sure that she was hoping I could find some. Finally, I responded with a simple truth: "Yes, it is."

Only a few moments had passed between her text and my response, but the door that her simple statement opened in my mind would usher in countless hours of thought and meditation regarding the meaning and content of my own life. My life had been hard. Struggles with mental health, rejection, low self-esteem, and a distorted idea of self-value carried me into and through experiences that stay with me, their lessons etched into the person I have become. My life has also been infinitely beautiful. I have encountered circumstances that forced me to see beyond my hurt in order to keep moving, and I discovered that I am a treasure. I have lost so much—things and people that I trusted and thought I needed—that I learned to acknowledge the boundless grace that saturated my days. And I've had enough moments of deep loneliness that my heart learned to recognize and appreciate fellow travelers divinely gifted to walk with me and encourage me along my way.

Though my life was hard at times, I hope my daughter is gifted with the wisdom I gathered along my way. I pray she will feel the truth of her existence extend beyond her personal experience because she encounters God's presence. I pray she will recognize the stepping-stones that are created in her life out of her most difficult moments. I pray she will experience the comfort of a friend's hand quietly slip into hers as she, inevitably, grieves loss or suffers humiliation.

That text exchange was not the last time my daughter would send me a message that confirmed her status as an adult. The next time, however, I was ready with a *but*. I was ready to provide her with the answer that gives shape and purpose to the struggles life brings us.

"Yes, life is hard. But God is good, grace abounds, and girlfriends are one of life's best gifts."

GOD

CHAPTER 2

MOMMY

I was once unbroken. / A complete idea / Sound in promise and purpose / Light and matter in harmony. / Then, I was born

My mother was an amazing person. I know that this is a commonly shared sentiment held by most sons and daughters when reflecting on their mothers and the lives they led. And it is true for most mothers. But my mother's amazingness is uniquely contoured to and for my heart and the hearts of my siblings. For us, she was it: the pattern, the place, the wonder. Her life was the shelter that protected us until we were smart enough to protect ourselves. She was the voice of discipline and kindness, in harmony, forming our character and conscience. She was the embrace that pushed us forward into the unknown with just enough confidence to stay in motion. The love we received from her was not soft and consuming, but it was supportive and substantive. It told us we are okay, while encouraging us to search for the truth of who we are. She was . . . amazing.

The memories I have of my mother are rich, weighty, and warm. Though she has been gone for more than ten years now, the colors that create the many anchor-points of my time with her have not faded. They are thick and animated, offering me moments where I can close my eyes and feel the soft smallness of her hand or hear the calm certainty of her voice. The many life-settling lessons she spoke to me still echo through the halls of my being daily. *It'll all work out; be careful how you treat people; get out of yourself.* These reminders to be bigger and kinder than I feel continue to illuminate my internal path, urging me to be better.

The impact my mother had on the lives of her children cannot be quantified or measured. She left a deep impression of her image and manner in each of our lives and the lives of our children. "You look just like your mother" has been said to each of us at one time or another. And we are forever accusing each other of "acting like Barbara Jean!" My brother, Sherman, inherited her musical talent. My niece Cassandra's hands are an exact replica of hers, while my daughter Jamyla's no-

nonsense approach to relationships was also inherited from her. One looks like her, while the other speaks with her phrasing and tone. Still another will set her frame in a way that mirrors mom's attitude or disposition. We bear witness to her life, in refrain, with each generation.

While there are so many lovely characteristics to recall about my mother, in truth, she was very human. And knowing her meant to know that humanity. The shadows of her struggles were not completely extinguished by the light. They were a part of her too. And we felt the loss of warmth whenever we unknowingly intruded on the broken areas of her life. Her journey was punctuated by poignant moments of loss and hurt. Hurt that was so light-altering that a large part of what I know about her was born from these traumas. And, as is all too common, the source of that hurt was the same resource from which she would attempt to draw from in hope of love.

For me, it is easy to remember my father only in terms of my mother's pain. Yet, my older siblings have a very different idea of him. For them he was a protector, a provider, and a teacher. He was smart and funny with a wide heart. He was charismatic with a curiosity about the people and world around him. And, oh man! Could he terrify the boys! Every boy in town knew the drill when it came to dating one of his girls: get out of the car and introduce yourself, remove your hat, and use mister and misses when addressing him or his wife. Yes, his stature was barely five feet and eight inches, but his voice was as firm as concrete and he kept a shotgun visible in the back window of his pickup truck.

The daddy I knew still carried whispers of these virtues. And my younger sisters, who experienced him under the same circumstances as I did, can remember family trips to the community pool, where he was a playmate and entertainer. They remember silly daddy and funny daddy. And those memories, though not easily recalled or detailed, live in me too. They just have little color or life for me. They are flat and hazy, faded out by more unpleasantly vivid ones.

I was not his favorite. Far from it. He didn't like me, and I knew this from a very young age. I could always sense his labored tolerance of me. I remember only a cold, rage-edged energy present in every interaction with him. I learned to practice a careful quiet when around him, anxious about what might happen otherwise. I have no warming memories of his arms around me in affection, no memory of his voice speaking the affirmation I so desperately needed. I was afraid of him, I longed for him, and I resented him. His insufficient love for me left holes in my self-image that I still contend with today. And those holes were stretched unreasonably large by witnessing his treatment of my mother and having to integrate those truths into my identity.

Writing page after page to detail and demonstrate the wounds my father imposed on me or my mother would serve no high purpose. It is enough for me to say that I was hurt. My pain was real, and I am here because of, and in spite of, it. What is most important is that I recognize why I was hurt. It has taken me years to understand that my hurt was not the result of anything I did or was. It was merely my father's attempt to displace his own pain. The injury he suffered at the hands of his abusive father, coupled with his mother's abandonment, hollowed out deep reservoirs that overflowed with pain, disappointment, and rage in his young soul, a fount he carried with him most of his life. He was hurt. He hurt me. And I was not the only one he hurt. There are pinpoints of pain scattered throughout my family because of the indignities and injuries my dad endured, and inflicted.

Yet, while she and I sat in the middle of that pain, wisdom was produced.

The wisdom and guidance I received from my mother was born from her days in her marriage. Now that I am older, I marvel at all that she withstood. The sheer volume of children she had to mother is awe-inspiring! She held the responsibility for the well-being of eleven souls. I am the mother of one, and

I often find my essence dangerously depleted by the emotional, spiritual, and physical needs of my daughter. How does one do that eleven times? Compound that with the fact that nine were girls, and it seems an impossibility. Then, add a broken heart.

My mother's heart was broken during my whole life. And, while my current memories of her are softened and colored by hindsight and the heaviness I still carry from her loss, I do not deny the scars that I bear from the wounds she received. My father shoveled heaps of self-worth from her with his blatant, repeated, public infidelity and dishonesty. He scattered the rich soil of her happiness to the four winds, depleting her emotions over the years. She had no choice but to place a protective layer of lukewarm remoteness between her heart, her feelings, her sanity, and him. And, by default, her children. And this produced unfortunate collateral damage that, ultimately, became ours to sift through.

There was an inaccessibility to my mother. She was always there and always available, but I never felt like I knew her (the deeper parts of her), and I never felt known by her. I spent my time as a young girl trying to figure out how to overcome a distance that I could not define and didn't understand. I craved her acknowledgement and confirmation. I studied her, trying to know what brought her joy or made her proud so that I could serve this to her. But I was rarely successful. There are moments buried inside of me that I treasure where it was just me and her, and she smiled at me or laughed with me. And my heart would expand in hope. But these moments are few. And the space in between is filled with the fear that I was not worth more.

The distance I struggled through in my relationship with my mom is real. But it is not everything. It is not close to everything. The amazingness that I described in the opening sentences is no less true. Contrarily, the details of her struggle provide evidence of her strength of character and dignity. Her life-story proved that our hearts can be broken and we can still be patient and caring, funny and kind. The mechanisms that she used to survive the damage done to her heart did not extinguish her brilliance. She still shined, and her light illuminated what was true about her. I knew she cared for me deeply. I knew she worried over me and wished good for me. And, what was most evident about my mother is this: I knew she prayed for me.

There is an old congregational song by gospel artist Dorothy Norwood that can still be heard reverberating through the walls of many African American churches on Sunday mornings. The lyrics are:

Somebody prayed for me / Had me on their mind / Took the time and prayed for me / I'm so glad they prayed, I'm so glad they prayed / I'm so glad they prayed for me.

How wonderful! Knowing that, as you come and go, making choices and dealing with consequences, there is someone who thinks well enough of you to lift your name to the heavens is empowering! It can give you the courage and ambition to move from one moment into the next.

Watching my mother through the years was a study in prayer and conviction. I cannot describe her without beginning and ending with her devotion to her faith and her unrelenting belief in and dependence on God. Her day started in prayer and Bible study and ended on her knees, again, in prayer. Every ordeal that came her way was whittled into manageable chunks by prayer. Her prayer time gave her the space she needed to feel her emotions without fearing that she would be consumed by them. She could confess her unhappiness, anger, and worries in confidence and freedom—no judgment and no shame. But she could also recover her joy and confirm her peace through prayer.

Put plainly: prayer is communication. However, learning the true value and purpose of prayer is a challenging process. While it is the single most important part of growing and developing as believers, it can also be the least understood. Prayer is not magic. It is not for emergency use only. It is not meant to be kept in a vault, brought out on occasion as an answer to a life crisis. It is not meant to be reflexive, and it should not be superficial. Prayer is crucial to a walk in faith. It is life-giving and lifting. It is clarity, counsel, and communion. It is practical, productive, and personal. It simultaneously elevates our perspective above constraints while grounding our thoughts in truth. It provides the substance of a relationship with Christ. Yet, the most common error many believers make on their growth path is to not prioritize prayer.

It is so easy to recognize the need for communication in our earthly relationships. An open exchange of thoughts is essential to any connection we want to keep and grow. For instance, many marital troubles are due to a lack of communication. If you browse the self-help aisle of any bookstore, you will find a wide variety of published works that aspire to help couples understand their needs and to communicate them to one another. If you go a week or even a day without speaking to your spouse, the dynamics of the marriage can shift. Even more importantly, if you allow your communication to become stilted and routine, you will soon feel the passion in your relationship fading. And, before you know it, what was once solid and sure becomes brittle and fragile. Someone you thought you knew intimately becomes an outsider. When communication stops, a dying process begins in the relationship that can only be rekindled by chancing the vulnerability that is necessary to start a simple, honest conversation.

The gift of prayer offers us a space for vulnerability. It is an opportunity to communicate directly to God. No pretense, no rejection, no fear. The God who created the heavens and formed the earth has a heart that longs to hear our voices sincerely reaching for Him. He revealed this desire when He walked with Adam in the garden, met Moses on the mountaintop, and listened to Jesus in the Garden of Gethsemane. And I had the privilege of witnessing the continuation of this revelation with my mother.

There is this image of my mother that all of her children hold dear. She is playing the piano during a church service. Her eyes are closed, and tears are streaming down her cheeks. Sometimes she sang while she played, other times she just provided the music for the songs of other voices. At all times, her heart poured into her fingers as both tribute and sacrifice. And, even in memory, that image provokes reverence. We had the honor of witnessing as she submitted herself to God as an offering and a prayer.

To one who didn't know her, the picture I paint of my mother can seem contradictory. I longed to have my personality and presence affirmed by her my whole life. At the same time, she was the warmest, most kind, honest person I have ever known. My kinship to her anchored and validated me. I was her daughter, and I felt grander because I could claim her as my own. However, my worst pain and regret from my time with her is that I did not get to know her better. I could not know her more. And though these two realities do not seem totally reconcilable, they are. Together they create a kaleidoscopic representation of my mother, with a very distinct and clear center. Her life was self-protection and pain. It was joy and deep disappointment. She suffered loss and humiliation, yet she was secure and assured. Her days were often filled with challenge, yet her life was lived as a prayer. She did not use religion as a life raft; she made her faith the foundation of her very existence. She was not perfect; she made mistakes. But she made sure that I inherited what was most valuable to her: a relationship with Christ. He was her center. And, with Him, her life—her whole life—was a beautiful portrait of grace and love in the face of pain and suffering. And her greatest desire was that each of her children partnered with Him to create their own likeness, one they could pass on to their children.

My mother's life was a wonderful example of what it means to serve God—although, for those looking from the outside, it may not have looked like it. She lived in the poverty-stricken area of a small, small-minded Midwestern town. She suffered the indignities that came with being a black woman in a white man's world. She mothered eleven children, each coming with their own challenges. She mothered while nursing a broken heart. Her friendship circle was small, and the wounds life had given her birthed barricades that kept others from getting too close. Even still, she created deep impressions of kindness, love, and generosity in the lives she touched, the depths of which rivaled what you might see in the most privileged life. Her kindness was relentless in spite of trauma and disappointment. Her love was not hot and emotional, but a constant temperature of compassion, truth, and quiet forgiveness. Her generosity was not contingent on the state of her storehouse and was carried out without reservation or resentment. She instilled in us an understanding of how important it is to live a life of meaning that produces blossoms in places that others cannot always see.

Because of the example my mother set, I now have my own relationship with Christ. Her belief in God's love and affection for her birthed a curiosity in me that could only be satisfied by my own encounter with Him. She tried His word and found it to be true and reliable. And I saw her trust Him. And he never failed her. He continually gave her beauty for ashes, and I am humbled to know that I was a part of that exquisite gift. God's presence helped her make sense of the many fractured parts of her life. And, throughout my own life-course, I am forever learning that only He can make sense of it all for me too.

CHAPTER 3

LOVE

Offer your heart / not to be used by man in his ignorance / but offer your heart / as match and candle. / Let love light you / from the inside out / and know: you are brilliant

God loves you. This is such a simple phrase. The entire message of the gospel wrapped up in three words. The phrase is small in word count but great in stature. It is the launching pad that takes us into authentic relationship with Christ.

God's love is declared countless times on Sunday mornings from pews and pulpits great and small. We sing songs and teach Sunday school lessons that reaffirm His love. We offer His love as a solution to our troubles and to encourage us toward higher ground while anchoring us to the bedrock of our faith. His love is presented to us in John 3:16 as a universal truth, and then it is condensed to a single point for us personally in John 15:13. He died, not just for the world, but for each of us. For me. For you.

The love of the creator is the birthright of every human being. Each of us was shaped, in affection and with purpose, to be an expression of His perfect love in our circumstances. You are valuable to Him, and He loves you. Profoundly, deeply, consistently, dependably, unconditionally, He loves you. He loves you in and out of seasons, through change and during stability. He loves you uncovered and hidden, empty and fruitful, yielded and unresponsive. He loves what you see as unlovable about you as well as the parts of you held dear and celebrated as special. He loves you inside out, through and through. He loves you.

Love is the most crucial component of life for the believer and non-believer alike. A person's understanding of and relationship with the idea of love shapes her world. If love has seemed lacking and illusive in your life, then your outlook will be overshadowed by thoughts of lack, hurt, offense, calamity, and emptiness. On the other hand, if you believe your life is filled with love, your perspective will assume abundance, security, and confidence. Most times, however, our lives are not shaped solely from one point of view or the other. It's rare that we go through our formative years without having seasons where we think we lack love and seasons where we think we have all the love we need. It's seldom all or nothing. Consequently, most people have a Swiss-cheese-like experience of love where they are whole in some places and broken in others.

What is true for the love journey, though, is not what we have grown accustomed to accepting. Love, as the world describes it, is a variable, often unattainable high that we chase through physical or emotional connection, momentary and fleeting. Or it is a mountain of obligation and landmines that we navigate in order to fulfill the necessary requirements. Or it's the blanket of comfort we attempt to wrap our lives in, too thin to protect us from the elements or so thick that we feel overwhelmed and smothered. Love, as the world offers it, is inconsistent, unreliable, teasing, and burdensome. It is never enough. And, yet, in order to obtain it, we must dissect it, categorize it, and break it down into bite-size, consumable pieces. We make it small. We reject the true potency of love and settle for a diluted haze-producing elixir—too sweet to digest and too weak to be sufficient. An over-used word of declared lust and fitful giddiness, the word love has become a tool of convenience instead of what it is. The error is that we limit our desire for love by conforming to how the world defines it. According to 1 John 4:16b, however, God is love, and, all who live in love, live in God and God lives in them. This is the only love that is more than enough, larger than everything.

For the believer, our relationship with God is the experience of Love. Knowing Him, recognizing His presence, and opening our hearts to Him is an ever-revealing ascension into love. It is not inconsistent. It is sure. It is not elusive. It is present and available. It is not weak. It is pure, potent, and effective. God's love is not expressed through splitting and categorizing based on emotional and physical need. It is simple, clear, defined. Love is patient, and Love is kind. Love is not jealous or boastful or proud or rude. Love does not demand its own way. It is not irritable, and it keeps no record of being wronged. It does not rejoice about injustice but rejoices whenever the truth wins out. Love never gives up, never loses faith, is always hopeful, and endures through every circumstance. When all is said and done, faith, hope, and love abide. But the greatest of these is love. (1 Corinthians 13)

Assessing and measuring our lovability and our access to love is our unconscious quest. There is not a moment in our days when we are not gauging the presence and availability of love. Connecting with our loved ones, engaging with our coworkers, and interacting with the strangers we meet on the street are all tentative tests, our way of checking for access to love. With our insecurities, we extend parts of ourselves forward to be judged, always hoping we will be found worthy of love. We dress ourselves up, painted and posed, smiling and witty, and wander the world with our subconscious screaming, "Please love me!"

We place our fears and pain behind a mask of activity and go in search of the next someone who will say, "Yes, you are worthy. I will love you." And if, by chance, we find a soul desperate enough to reach back, we soon learn that he, too, is searching for love. We are, each of us, fractured vessels, aimlessly searching for what we think we want, putting our hope in a thing that bears a striking resemblance to ourselves.

My pursuit of love took me into common places. Anxiety, promiscuity, and fear are familiar benchmarks in every woman's hunt for love. We, not yet sure we are whole, place our souls on the open market, vainly hoping a man will come along with the right materials needed to finish our incomplete identities. This fruitless venture begins long before we are even aware that we are travelers and a journey is underway. It begins in empty places, where we are taught to write loneliness in the shape of a heart. We are taught that love is a feeling, something we fall into that steals our sense and our senses. It robs us of our reason and hides logic far away. We are taught to long for love and search for its source in the faces around us. And we are told that, when we find love, we will know that it is love, because our heart—that deceitful, desperately wicked thing that we cannot know—will testify. (Jeremiah 17:9)

On my journey, I was subconsciously trying to find someone who could help me make sense of the missing parts of my self-image, those holes created by the dysfunctional interactions I had with my father. The mental image I had of myself was comically disfigured. My body image, the makeup of my personality, and the purpose of my womanhood was a mangled, incomplete puzzle that often grieved and exhausted me. Clothes, makeup, drama, and sex were the bandages I used to cover the wounds in my soul.

During my younger years, my life consisted of a series of games with men where I would show them one piece of my fragmented self-image, followed by another, just to see how much they would be willing to accept before showing signs of fear or disgust. Before they would leave. I never expected them to stay very long. Still, with sex, emotion, and a slow reveal, I tried to stretch out their interest long enough that I could rest from the search, if only for a short while. The catch was this: Their willingness to stay was never long enough and always too long. My father-history told me I was intolerable, unlikeable. I would never be pretty enough, smart enough, enough-enough to keep a man engaged. Besides that, I was afraid and disgusted by the image of myself drawn on the walls of my mind. So their willingness to accept any part of me for any length of time would wedge me into a confined mental space where I was caught between gratitude and anger—grateful for their ability to accept me even with my ever-expanding list of defects, and angry that the gaps in their standards were so large that they allowed space for someone like me.

When trying to recall the details of my many efforts to attain love through romantic means, I usually end up with fuzzy images and sketchy details. Sometimes I can remember a name but not a place or an occasion but nothing beyond that. What I do recall are the feelings that drove me through that period of time. Every relationship I had as a young woman was designed by fear, filled with insecurity, and edged with desperation. Though I pretended, I never found real satisfaction or contentment, and I always left measuring at least an ounce emptier than when I entered. While in this depleting cycle, I married a stranger (it'd only been a few months since our meeting) and birthed my daughter. I, subsequently, separated from him, found other relationships before I was divorced, and attempted to start the cycle again. Then, my life was overtaken by mind-shifting mercy in the shape of depression. Depression so deep that I lost my ability to pretend.

Creating a palatable image for those around us can be an all-consuming undertaking. Whether for a man or a friend, for our family or our community, wondering and worrying about how we are perceived by others can take over our thoughts. Unconsciously, we interrogate ourselves regarding how we are perceived by others. Anxieties like "Do they like me," "Do they think I'm smart," "Am I too fat or too thin," become a constant part of our thought-life. They slither through our minds randomly and, before long, if left unchecked, turn into our primary focus.

Once, I went to a nightclub in a lacy, see-through top without a bra. I know this may not be a big deal for some. Clothing choice doesn't always tell a story. However, for me, this one act exposed the truth of my primary longing at that time. I wanted to be seen, and I wanted to be loved. But, I felt unseen and unlovable. So unlovable that I was willing to overthrow my conservative nature and expose myself for attention and possible affection. From the moment I looked at myself in the mirror, I was uncomfortable and felt obscene. But my yearning to be seen and loved screamed so loudly in my head that my spirit—the part of me that tells me I am enough, I am lovable without a see-through top—was drowned out. So, there I was, sitting on a barstool in a club, in my twenty-year-old skin and body, with dignity and desperation struggling for dominance inside of me. And all it took was for one man to give me one moment for dignity to be overcome. From that moment forward, I would do whatever it took to keep that attention as long as I could. Even if it meant that years later I still cringe when thinking about it.

To paint what we think is a desirable public picture of ourselves, we arbitrarily reach for and arrange random characteristics into strategic shapes—though we are usually not sure if what we are reaching for is really what we want to be. For example, we want to be smart and sexy but approachable and relatable, kind but formidable, and compassionate but not overly emotional. For me, this is already too much. Just the effort to be sexy overwhelms me! Because what does that mean? We call everything from our toes to our attitudes sexy. And with such an ambiguous definition, how can anyone clearly absorb the idea of sexiness for herself? Does it mean that you're appealing in a strictly sexual way? (Well, I don't want that . . . do I?) Does it mean that you are more womanly than the women around you? Are extensions and red lips enough, or do I need six-inch heels and a waist trainer as well? I am sure that if I asked six different women what it means to be sexy, I would get six different answers. One would point to her clothes; another would reference her hair; and someone else would say it is in the attitude or intelligence. Yet, however we choose to define it, we are never enough of it.

I am still amazed at how willing I was to compromise my mental stability to get the approval of men by trying to become someone I was not in order to be what I thought they wanted. It became a pattern in my life for too many years. I would desperately compromise any progress I had made in figuring out who I was in order to get the approval of a man, and the effort would only end in disappointment and regret. And with each round of this, a layer of my self-esteem was stripped away. I finally, and gratefully, lost the ability to pretend to be anything other than what I was: broken and depressed.

Being stripped to the rawest form of myself was indescribably painful and, surprisingly, freeing. While I had no choice but to confront my behavior and the brokenness behind it, I was also released from being concerned about what others thought of me. I was flattened, and all of my energy had to be redirected toward rising. I agreed to be hospitalized, hoping the doctors could help me. And they did, inasmuch as they could, by encouraging me to negotiate the darkness. But I craved light, though I didn't know this at the time. I burned inside to not just be relieved, but to be changed. Light dawned when I gained the courage to ask God if I could ever really be loved. In my broken state, with a shattered image, I asked God, Am I lovable? And

He answered by expanding the fragrant presence of His love inside of me.

It took a long time for me to gain a healthy understanding of love. Yet, I am still surprised by how His love is revealed in new ways for me each day. In my most challenging moments, His love is there to relieve my burden. However, the fact that love shows up is not the point. God is love. He is also omnipresent. Therefore, love is always present. God and His love don't show up—not really. God and His love are always there and have always been there. I only had to recognize that. And that is where the miracle lives. We experience the wonder of God's love when we can finally wade through all of the false ideas, the moments of rejection and hurt, the lustful urgings, the unrealistic images, and experience His presence in our innermost darkness and hidden parts. And in that moment, we begin to be understand real love.

Here is what we should be taught about love: the substance of love is not discovered in a rapidly beating heart or a mind driven to tunnel vision and distraction. You will not happen upon it in a hazed-filled lust. And it will not find you and declare your perfection. Love is steady, waiting for you with hope and expectation, as you move forward at a turtle's pace, learning the lessons life has for you: that's patience. Love is holding your hand, even in the midst of your offensiveness, extending the kind of grace that cuts through your pain: that's kindness. Love stands rooted in His resolve to be with you, even when your heart has led you away into adulterous deeds. He is quiet in the triumph of your return, assuring you of your place with Him. He is a gentleman, encouraging you toward your next place of abundance. He endures without record and rejoices in the dawning of your understanding. He never gives up, and He never loses hope. He is not a hidden object or an abstract puzzle that must be solved to be attained. Love is not something you search for; He is someone you acknowledge.

He is here. What we look for, what we long for, what we hope for is Him. For God so loved us that He gave us the perfection of His love in the person of His son—Himself—upon a cross. And He demonstrated the purpose and power of that love by rising up, from humiliation, devastation, and loss. And in this demonstration, we are taught that this power—to rise and conquer—lives in us too. Love is God. And we who dwell in Him dwell in love.

CHAPTER 4

MIRACLE

When we break / we create space in our darkness / for Light to abide.

Have you ever watched the ocean from a beach? Witnessed the waves gently giving way to one another as they travel to and fro? Or watched the sun's rays splinter into a rainbow just before meeting the ocean's glassy surface? Looking out onto the seemingly endless spread of undulating water is sure to provoke even the most jaded, rigid heart into a condition of awe and wonder.

The ocean appears to go on and on, all the way to the eye's limit and beyond. Not to mention the depth of it. Down, down, down! Far beyond our realm of thought or dream. The world's tallest building stacked atop itself five times over would still be consumed by its deepest depths! It covers around seventy percent of the earth's surface, and, according to the National Oceanic and Atmospheric Administration (NOAA), we have explored less than ten percent of its body to date. When you consider the history of man—ingenuity, imagination, technological advances—it seems we should know the ocean better by now. Yet, there is a whole world carrying on in the ocean's depths of which we have no idea. There are life forms sustained and concealed by it—unique, beautiful creatures— our eyes may never see. Yet, the same ocean that houses these mysteries affects our everyday life on dry land. It has the power to drive weather patterns, regulate temperature, and support life. In its persistence and tenacity, it erodes mountainous boulders into grains of sand. The contours and curves of the earth's coasts are shaped and re-shaped by its power over and over again. Without it, our ability to transport goods, people, and other effects that are essential to keeping the wheels of the world economy turning would be blunted, and we would have a much more divided, isolated global society.

The power and mystery of the ocean are reflective of a much larger creation picture. The ocean is moved by the air; they collaborate to shape and nourish the land. The land shelters and nourishes the creatures that inhabit it. The creatures that inhabit the land take in the air and the water, nourishing and being nourished—being served in its beginning and serving in its end. The water, the land, the air, and the creatures all work together in synchronicity, fostering the continuation of all things. From their efforts we are protected and sustained and are able to experience unimaginable beauty along the way, in the most unexpected places, from the minute to the profound. The patterns on a butterfly's wings or on a ladybug's back, the fragrance of flowers and the swaying of tall grass in a field, the majesty of a mountain or the gentle crashing of the ocean's surf all have the power to overtake our emotions and broaden the horizon of our souls like nothing else.

I once visited a beach in Honduras. As the sun set, I sat in the sand and took in the beauty before me. The blueness of the ocean, contrasted against the shifting yellows, pinks, and oranges of the sun's rays traveling through the sky, was an amazing sight to witness. As the sun further descended and the brighter colors were consumed by darker hues, I closed my eyes and listened to the waves. They roared and hummed all at once, leading me into a place of peace and wellness. In that moment, I was infinitely important and inconceivably small. Strength and powerlessness, purpose and insignificance, love and loneliness all peacefully coexisted there, imbuing me with a sense of belonging that I had never experienced before. I was certain that my role in creation was simple but important, meaningful but not principal.

The balance and flow of creation is complex and awe-inspiring. It vibrates with creatures and mysteries, great and small. It is a perplexing, beautifully intricate life-web of which we are only a silken strand. It connects all of the parts in a divinely choreographed dance of need and provision that is beyond our comprehension. It hums and sings in harmony in praise to the creator.

In the Bible, Luke 19, there is a phrase that Jesus uses to address the Pharisees that has always provoked an acute response within me. It is in the re-counting of Jesus' arrival in Jerusalem, also known as the Triumphal Entry. Jesus is riding through the streets of Jerusalem, and His disciples rejoice with loud voices. The Pharisees, who were offended by the praise and adoration being lavished on Jesus, told Him to rebuke them. Jesus then says, "I tell you that if these should keep silent, the stones would immediately cry out." Can you imagine! An object, on which we place little to no value, being used to help fulfill one of the most significant prophecies in history? And even beyond the rocks, there are other examples of creation rising up to support this moment, such as the donkey and the palm branches. Each time I read these verses, the unseen bond that I share with the rest of creation is revealed. I am a part of the priceless artistic expression of God's creativity and love: simultaneously static and changing, finished and in process.

Humanity joined in this creation dance to serve Jesus as He prepares to perform the greatest act of service in history.

A rock crying out sounds fantastic. There are rocks everywhere, and we have yet to see or hear of one creating sound by its own strength. From our perspective, there would be no reason for a rock to have a voice. Our egocentric logic says that the purpose of a rock is concretely established only by its service to man. Diamonds, rubies, onyx, and marble have value because we say they do, and we cannot imagine that they could be used beyond what we have determined. Why would these objects ever need to speak? Yet, Jesus, who could have said, the children or animals or the wind and trees, purposely refers to the rocks—objects that are totally devoid of the ability to independently make sound. Furthermore, the reference to the rock is not the first time this happened in the Bible. Scripture constantly uses nature to advance a great purpose by using it outside of its commonly accepted place in our understanding or ability. A burning bush instructed Moses to go to Egypt to deliver His people, and the Red Sea became their escape. A cloud was their guide through the wilderness, and a mountain was a sacred space where Moses met with God.

God endows generic objects with exceptional qualities throughout the Bible, but many people, scholars and believers alike, have described these narratives as symbolic or allegorical. "Of course a rock couldn't cry out," they would declare in their quest to make scripture palatable. "Jesus was using the rock to express the passion His disciples felt at that moment." Because, although we want to believe in Jesus, we want to stay grounded in reality. Right? Yet, one can't help but wonder how we can embrace Jesus, whose recorded life on earth was steeped in the miraculous, if we can't embrace the possibility of miracles.

Imagine: Jesus is God wrapped in flesh. He put on humanity so that He could sacrifice Himself for Himself in order to reconcile His creation to Himself. This foundational fact is the starting block for our introduction to Jesus. We must embrace this truth in order to embrace His earthly purpose and the inscrutable plan and power of salvation. Yet, the mystery is already beyond the capacity of our mortal understanding. Therefore, it is impossible to accept the truth of Jesus without first making peace with the presence of the miraculous. Beginning with Mary receiving a visitation from the Angel of the Lord and the Immaculate Conception, to the use of the star as a marker for His birthplace, all the way through to His death and resurrection, the supernatural is consistently present in Jesus' story. Blinded eyes and deaf ears are opened, health is restored to the sick, the dead is raised, crippled limbs are repaired, thousands are fed with a meal meant for one, storms are calmed, and mental health is renewed. Miracles are the vehicle that drive Jesus from the womb to the cross. Yet, by reducing Him into a dimension that is intellectually manageable for us, we limit our ability to fully lean into the truth of who He is. Furthermore, it diminishes our ability to understand fully who we are.

A video circulating on social media detailed the human life development process prior to birth. It followed the transformation of a baby from conception through the entirety of gestation. I watched it. It was breathtaking. I was mesmerized by the depiction of the changes that take place between fertilization and birth. The fertilized cell splits repeatedly as it morphs into a form that resembles a tadpole. A heartbeat appears, appendages sprout, dark orbs take shape on the head as eyes begin to form, ears emerge, fingers push forward, and a mouth becomes visible. In just a few months, it is easy to discern the tiny object as a burgeoning human. It begins to move in the womb as it practices using its new limbs. The mother feels the quickening of life inside of her, and it isn't long before she sees the proof of it as little bumps appear and disappear on her belly's surface. So many fantastic processes take place in perfect sequence as another life is prepared to impact the world. This body that could live for seventy-five years or more is shaped and equipped for natural life in just about forty weeks.

Watching that video gave me such an appreciation for the physical development of humans. Witnessing human ontogenesis inspired a respect for the many doctors and nurses who dedicate themselves to facilitating the health and wellness of such a complicated structure with so many intricately elaborate systems. But, even as it heightened my admiration for science, it also inspired depth in my faith. How can we not acknowledge the miraculous in the life development process? The beautiful blossoming of a small human inside of a human is, alone, a wonder. Yet, it is just a single layer of what makes a person who he is. What about the evolution from seed to soul? How do we become uniquely ourselves?

Look at your hands and remember the many times you've used them to comfort a loved one. Grab a mirror and gaze into your eyes. Think of all of the sights you've seen in your lifetime. Consider every word you've ever spoken that has healed or encouraged another. Imagine the highway of arteries running through your body that feed your heart and organs with your life's blood. Now consider that it all started with a fertilized egg and a splitting cell. One moment triggered a complex, mysterious process, and you are here—not just physically but spiritually.

When my daughter was an infant, I used to lay with her in

my arms, her face to my face. I would stare at her for hours in awe. My eyes would outline every curve and slope. Her perfect little nose and mouth, her sweet, round cheeks and tiny chin. What a miracle. However, what was most amazing about that experience was how fully my daughter was herself from the moment I met her. There was a quality to her that distinguished her as her own. She was more than another baby. She was more than my daughter. She was a matchless expression of unique energy and awareness fitting an ethereal space that only her essence could fill. Here physical form shared commonalities with others of her age, gender, and size, but her substance, her spiritual presence could not be duplicated or substituted by another.

The most exquisite part of my interaction with her was that I had this deep knowing of her. She was my baby. I could sense her moods and needs, I knew how to give her comfort, and she was never more content than when I held her in my arms. She was unique and dear and worthy in every way. Her sweet little personality was evident in her from the start. Observant, determined, kind, and thoughtful. I knew her, and watching her grow was like witnessing the flowering of a rose. There was no doubt it would be beautiful, I just wasn't sure how the petals would choose to express that beauty.

There is an intangible element that is primary to defining who you are. Your quintessence cannot be fully captured through a description of your physical attributes. You are more. You are your thoughts and feelings, your beliefs and convictions, and your preferences and desires. No one else sees the world like you do, and no one else understands the nuances of life from your viewpoint. Your life will fill spaces and touch people in a way that no one else can. And this "you," this rareness, this exceptionality, existed before your physical development began.

A story in the Old Testament tells us about a prophet named Jeremiah. He was the young son of a priest who served in the land of Benjamin. About six hundred years before the coming of Christ, God called Jeremiah to minister to His people. God tells Jeremiah, "Before I formed you in the womb I knew you, before you were born I set you apart; I appointed you as a prophet to the nations." (Jeremiah 1:5) This intimate interaction between God and Jeremiah is so poignant. Jeremiah, young and insecure, has this moment with God where he is affirmed in person and purpose. Like I knew my daughter, God knew Jeremiah. He speaks to Jeremiah's destiny, but he also emphasizes that Jeremiah was known to God since the man's inception and that he was formed with a distinct plan and purpose.

This moment between God and Jeremiah speaks to the deepest desire that every person holds. We all crave to be known and valued and to know that there is a plan and we have purpose. And through this exchange, we are satisfied. Before we were formed, we were known, and God shaped us to play a very specific part in His eternal plan. In your pre-physical state, God was holding you in His arms, staring into your eyes, and speaking purpose. Pause and let that truth settle over you. You are known. You have a role in creation that is specific to you. The knowing of you began before the genesis of your physicality, and your purpose has been a part of you from the beginning.

I often counsel my daughter through her crisis moments. Most of the time, these climatic occasions are brought about through rejection, a lack of appreciation, or a failed attempt to move into a new space. It quakes the foundations of certainty of her destiny and has her questioning her value and direction. Her purpose becomes an external target that she is chasing and trying to keep in focus. I listen quietly, remembering how sure she seemed when she lay in my arms all those years ago. Often, I become overwhelmed with the urge to shout to her, "Daughter! That is not purpose. Quit chasing it, for you are purpose!"

At the same time, I wonder how we lose it. How does this potency of belief and certainty fade, leaving us in a condition where our physical presence is dominant in our identity and purpose is external to our being? Somewhere along our way, we lose sight of our soul and limit ourselves based on our bodies. We allow ourselves to become no more than what is seen. Yet, what we see of people pales in comparison to who they fully are.

When you consider that what you are seeing from your viewpoint on any given beach is just a small fraction of the ocean, it amazes the mind and taxes the imagination to its limits. As far as your eyes can see, there is only water. And that, alone, seem huge. Yet, the fact of the entirety of the ocean is even larger than what you see and what you are experiencing. It stretches, in scope and purpose, miles beyond your horizon. It is larger than what you can take in given the limits of your physical body. How foolish it would be for us to believe that what we are seeing is the end of the ocean! This goes doubly so for humanity. What we see of ourselves and of others is a whisper of the beginning of our true presence.

The truth of our existence is rooted in the miraculous. Your presence and your impact are not confined by the tangible. Your substance—the core of who you are—did not begin in the moments following fertilization. There is no organic mechanism responsible for your spiritual quickening, and we began long before we were birthed into the natural world. Yet, we often use our flesh in our attempt to grasp the fullness of who we are.

We use a scientific approach, like NOAA with the ocean, in our attempt to know, fully, who we are. We explore ourselves piece by piece in hope that we will unearth a key that unlocks a fuller understanding. But we are not the ocean; we are the miracle. The ocean seems unending. Yet, it is finite—there is a coast on the other side. The ocean is large, but its depths are calculable. The ocean can influence the weather and the temperature, but it cannot command it. It can erode a mountain over time, but it cannot move it. And when the earth passes away, the ocean does too. Your beginning is the image of God, and you are an expression of his love. We are a part of the eternal. Before our flesh was formed, our being was breathed, and, when our flesh ends, our souls will continue. We appear finite; yet, we are eternal. Our depth and breadth cannot be naturally defined. We are the embodied purpose of an all-knowing, ever-present, all-powerful God who speaks peace to the wind, shuts up the heavens on command, and moves mountains in response to the tiniest bit of our faith. The ocean, in all of its greatness, is nothing in comparison to the miracle that is you.

GRACE

CHAPTER 5

AWAKENING

How lovely are these wounds! / I have covered them / afraid the details would pull me under / But they are good / power and light / breaking through my thickest, darkest night.

I was never on time for work. Regardless of how short or long the commute to my place of employment, I would always manage to arrange my morning routine so that I was at least two minutes late. Gratefully, most of the places where I worked over the years had conveniently ignored this flaw—everyone has flaws! Besides, once I was there, I more than made up for the two- to fifteen-minute time violation by zealously committing to the various tasks under my responsibility. On top of that, I had developed a great deal of technical skill and aptitude throughout my many years working in various industries and office environments, which made me a great problem solver. Everywhere I was employed, I was presented with the opportunity to impress the powers that be with my ability to meet some emergent need at some critical point. So, why would my insufficiency in personal time management matter when I was always proving myself indispensable in so many other areas? For many years, it didn't.

In the early millennium, my family and I relocated from Atlanta to Ohio. I'd spent years cultivating relationships of trust and accommodation with the company that I worked for in Atlanta, so the thought of finding a new job and starting the relationship-building process all over again was disheartening, to say the least. Yet, I forged ahead, put myself out there, and was hired by a Catholic women's organization to run their business office. These women were a part of an international congregation that focused on providing services to the poor and ignored of the societies in various parts of the world. My duty was to provide administrative support to the various Sisters and to assist the elected Minister with managing the various business processes for the United States area. For the first time in my experience as a believer, I was being afforded an opportunity to help provide for my household while simultaneously contributing to efforts of faith.

Even as I was nervous about starting over, I found myself excitedly anticipating becoming a part of the charity work and efforts of faith that these women performed. I am not Catholic, but I staunchly hold to the beliefs and teachings of Christ. Even though I was raised in a somewhat restrictive Pentecostal community of faith, my life journey had taught me the importance of looking beyond the legal tenets of the organized religious community that one is a part of in order to find the heart of that person. Christ is the common ground. Christ is the connecting point. With Christ as our agreed-upon point of reference, our paths are bound to merge and focus on a common destination. As long as I could see the bridge that Christ provided to the Father through the fog of denominational rhetoric, I knew that our journeys were parallel—regardless of differing viewpoints over the intent of one scripture or another. Underneath it all, we were all working toward a Kingdom agenda.

This meant for me that, by being given this position, I now had the opportunity to actively pursue the agenda of Christ without the restriction and reservation usually found in work environments. As a believer, what more could I want?

Immediately, I found a rhythm and comfort with the requirements for my new position in Ohio. They needed computer skills; I had those. They needed creativity; I had it. They needed writing skills; I had that. They needed someone to ensure the office was open on time in the morning . . .

For the first time in as many years as I could remember, my inability to arrive at work on time became a point of concern regarding my ability to meet my employer's expectations. My supervisor, I'll call her Janine, preferred that I arrive five minutes early to prep for the day before opening the office. I disappointed her immediately. Honestly, I never gave any consideration to arriving early. Any effort that I put toward getting to work in a timely manner was focused on meeting the official start time by mere seconds, if at all. Needless to say, even my half-hearted attempts never paid off. It wasn't long before my inability to meet the minimum requirement of arriving by the time the office was supposed to be open became a huge, silent point of contention between me and my supervisor. When I would walk in the office one minute after I was scheduled to be there, Janine would sometimes be standing next to my chair. I could see the tension seated in her shoulders as she pretended to review a document in her hands. On other mornings, she'd be hidden in her office, and I'd feel a cold, frustrated presence occupying an uncomfortable amount of space for hours after I arrived. With a look of utter frustration and confusion, she'd greet me in a flat-toned "Good morning" instead of asking the question that was obviously pressing on her mind: "Why are you always late!"

During that first year, I struggled consistently with being as close to on-time as possible. I got up, sometimes with plenty of time to complete my morning ritual and make it by the nine o'clock start time. Invariably, some issues would swallow my extra time, ensuring I arrived just beyond the moment I was expected. There was always some reason, some issue that seemed legitimate, that prevented me from making the start time. Maybe I noticed that the kitchen hadn't been tidied the night before, so I'd take a few minutes to clean before I left for work. Maybe the shoes I'd planned to wear that day weren't where they were supposed to be, forcing an extra ten minutes onto my preparation time. Sometimes I decided to eat breakfast or pack lunch just before I left, and sometimes I wanted to see the end of a morning news segment. Whatever the reason—and there always was one—I was late!

After many, many unspoken awkward mornings, Janine finally offered a compromise that should have solved our issue. She caught me just as I walked in the door one morning.

"Good morning, Sheila!" Her greeting was so upbeat and tension free that I stopped at the door and waited for her to explain her mood. "Come in and get settled. I want to have a chat."

"Okay." I was completely off balance. I'd grown used to the awkwardness and didn't know what to do without it. "Are you okay?"

"Yes, yes, I'm fine!" And she really did seem fine. "Let me know when you've settled."

Butterflies bounced around the walls of my stomach as I made my way to my desk and began the day's preparations. My nerve endings were sparking with anxiety. I knew, of course, that the conversation would be about my tardiness; it was way overdue. I just expected it to come in a different package. I spent a few minutes building my defense by reasoning in my mind that I was usually only late by a few minutes; no one was ever waiting in line for me to open the door; and that I more than made up for my tardiness in other areas. Most days I stayed late enough to make up for it anyway! Certainly she couldn't fire me over a few minutes? After I prepared my rebuttal, I let her know I was ready to chat.

Janine came in, sat, and immediately began reciting the many reasons why she appreciated me and what I offered to the organization. She was so sincere in her delivery that all the nervousness I initially felt melted into a strange mix of gratitude, pride, and shame. She told me about how sure she was that I was meant to be a part of their mission, because she'd prayed that God would send the right person before she interviewed me (gratitude). Never in a million years did she expect me to offer so much talent and giftedness to their efforts, and she was very pleased with how much I'd contributed to the ministry (pride). Having said all of that, she wanted us to come up with a solution to the strain and pressure the opening time for the office was putting on me (shame). She went on to say that she'd noticed that nine o'clock seemed to be a little too early for me and suggested that she would move the opening time back thirty minutes so that I would have plenty of time to get there without stress. And she did. She moved the opening time back 30 minutes. For me. So that I could be on time. And I was on time—for a few weeks. Eventually and unintentionally (so I thought), I adjusted my morning routine to the point that I was once again never on time. Eventually, Janine and I fell into a comfortable dance of silent resignation and disappointment.

On one particular morning months later, I was excited. I had finally left home early enough to make it to work on time! At my current timeline, I could get there, park, and be walking in the door by nine o'clock at the latest, and I was feeling good! I pulled into the parking lot near the back dock so that I could cut through the kitchen and possibly shave a few seconds off of my trek from the car to the office. I got out of my car and walked with purpose toward my destination. As I approached the dock, I noticed the cook, Anne, sitting on the steps enjoying a morning cigarette. My intention was to smile, say "hello" as I walked by on my way to being on time. I walked up the steps, never breaking my stride, and offered Anne my canned morning greeting with barely a glance in her direction.

"Good morning, Anne! How are you this morning?" I asked without ever intending to appreciate her answer—I was going to be on time!

"Hi, Sheila! I'm doing good! I feel really good!"

The levity in her voice caused me to pause against my will and look down into her face. Internally, curiosity and annoyance battled, because I knew I was wasting precious moments that would assure my need to speed walk through the building to my office in order to make my goal, but I'd been drawn in by the unusual tenor in her voice. As my eyes connected with her face, curiosity gained victory. My goal to be on time immediately slid down my priority list. Her face was filled with the evidence of a new characteristic, one I hadn't seen on her before that I couldn't quite name.

I'd seen Anne every day for the past year and had gotten

used to the sad heaviness that cloaked her whenever I encountered her. She shared various segments of her life's history with me, and it rehearsed the typical story of brokenness where the main character is steeped in poverty, struggling with unhealthy relationships, and generally adrift. Anne exuded negativity most times. At some point, I began to limit the amount of time I would spend in Anne's presence, simply because I knew me. There was a part of me that embraced negativity. Unfortunately, it was my natural go-to place. It supported the perversions that had taken root in my personality early on that nurtured depression and sadness. Through the small amount of self-examination that I had done, I became aware of this major truth, acknowledged it, and attempted to be mindful of it in my everyday interactions. Anne's disposition of pessimism triggered this tendency in me. Her fragmented relationship with her daughter, her overdue rent, her ailing car—if I allowed myself to have more than a fleeting curiosity about her story, a perpetually healing wound inside of me would beg for its attention, beckoning my own discontentment and depression. But the face I was staring into was not *that* Anne's face. She was different, changed somehow. She seemed new. And with sudden clarity I deciphered the characteristic that now seemed a natural part of her facial features. It was hope.

"Wow, Anne! You look wonderful." I was so overwhelmed by her transformation that I forgot about being on time and stood quietly and listened as she described what I knew would forever be the most significant moment in her life. My heart soared as I listened to her describe how much relief she'd felt when she'd consciously and intentionally chosen Christ.

"Relief," I'd repeated thoughtfully. That is such an appropriate word for that moment. Before choosing Christ, many of us don't recognize how much mental and spiritual effort we put into just trying to hold it together. We expend tremendous amounts of our limited energy and efforts attempting to manage our impossible external image against our frustrated, stressed internal image. Somewhere in childhood, we begin developing a mental checklist filled with our expectations for ourselves; then we overfill it with the expectations of others. A list like that is destined to be defeating! Think back to the state of your mental health at sixteen. Just considering revisiting that time of life can cause anxiety to awaken in many of us. We spent so much time trying to figure out who we were, our values and beliefs about the world around us and about ourselves, while trying to fit in with a group of peers struggling with the same insecurities. We developed a checklist of wants and desires, dos and don'ts chalked with unrealistic goals that we chased into adulthood. Yet most of us resign our lives to managing this unreasonable checklist. We spend our days trying to fulfill our desire for ourselves—balancing our good and successful against our missteps and mistakes—along with constantly trying to project the version of ourselves that is acceptable to those around us. It's an impossible, exhausting task!

The permission Christ gives us to detach from this list of all the issues that had somehow gained the power to rule our lives—who we think we are, who we are trying to be for others, the hurts, distortions, untruths, and plain misinformation—can only be described as relief! It is an instant shedding and letting go; a releasing that can never be compared to or replaced by any other life experience. It can have an instant effect on your countenance, as it had for Anne. As I listened to her, I was in awe of her experience—and maybe a little envious. I rejoiced for her and, at the same time, I realized how far I was from that place. So, I listened to Anne, in this confused state of happiness and internal discomfort, while, in the back of my thoughts, somewhere way behind my growing joy and curiosity about Anne's transformation, I knew that I would be late, again. Probably later than usual.

For weeks following my encounter with Anne, I was unsettled. I was, of course, joyful for Anne's salvation. I watched as she came and went from that day on, and I could see how her decision had affected the manner in which she played her part in the daily journey. Where there had once been a cloud of defeat that carried her through her days, there was now an openness, a willingness in its place. I watched with delight as she settled into the truth of who she *was not* and cautiously became acquainted with the newly developing image of herself. It was like watching a child who had discovered she could rise from a seated position and walk! She was no longer restricted to the view from the floor. A new reality was possible for her, and she was ready to venture it! Where she'd been comfortable diving into conversations of negativity, she would now stand quietly or walk away. Where she used to tell her story by highlighting all of her hardships and disappointments, she now focused on how hopeful she was that her difficult situations would improve and about how determined she was to do what it took to make those improvements happen. Anyone who witnessed her change couldn't help but feel joy as a natural by-product.

Yet, joy wasn't the only by-product I received from this experience. There was another unexpected and unwanted consequence. It was as if an internal wall that I didn't know existed had been breached, allowing whatever was being blocked off inside of me to push through. And it was relentless. My sleeping pattern was interrupted. My daily habits and routines were invaded. My ability to focus was overshadowed. It wouldn't go away. Still, I tried my best to ignore it. The more I tried to smother this irritating, almost painful, eruption taking place in me, the more insistent it became. After a while, I found myself sitting in the middle of a full-blown episode of depression. I was withdrawn, I was sad, I was hurting. And while I could vaguely link the beginnings of my situation to my encounter with Anne, I still couldn't identify the meaning of the connection.

So, I did the only thing I knew to do. I powered through. I went to work (late), I met my obligations with my family and friends (barely), and I occupied my thoughts with anything that would help me ignore (unsuccessfully) what had, at this point, taken over my spiritual and emotional life. Yes, I prayed about it, but my prayers were similar to the morning greetings I got from Janine when I walked in late. Her greetings were sufficient enough to force a small opening in our line of communication, but it never addressed the main issue: Why?

Janine was never willing to embrace the one uncomfortable moment that would come with asking the important question that could get her to the solution. There were just too many unknowns. What if I argued with her? What if I cried? What if I yelled or threw something? What if I quit? And for me, the unknowns were just as daunting. What if it hurt too much? What if it cost more than I could give? What if I was the problem? What if it was something I knew but didn't want to *know*? There were so many what ifs that, just like Janine, I was trapped into believing that avoiding the potential conflict was more

important than reaching a possible solution. I just wasn't willing to risk asking the questions, because I was afraid that the path to the solution was a journey that I couldn't handle. I was afraid the pain would be too much.

Eventually, I learned to manage my depression to the point that it was unrecognizable to most. I found a rhythm, and I lived in this spiritual inertia for years. I was functioning but numb and disconnected. I met my obligations, in as much as I could, and made sure that I still appeared to be "okay" to those around me—at least to those who didn't look close enough to notice the truth of my condition. Any energy I could conjure up from my empty stores would go towards just barely making it through my days.

For a long time, my only goal was getting from one day to the next, which removed Anne from my radar. So, I was alarmed and saddened when, by chance, I took note of her and noticed that her countenance had begun to dull. She was, once again, escorted by a heavy presence. The threatening shadow attending to her was different from the beast that had shrouded her in the past, but its presence had clearly altered her. The disappointment I felt was more intense than I ever expected it to be. I was sad, hurt, and, most of all confused.

How did she get back there? How did she have a *real* experience with Christ and end up spiraling back to where she'd come from? The more questions surfaced, the more I edged toward anger. My anger shifted restlessly at the boundary of my emotions dying to ask the question that had become the ultimate taboo for me. It was the question that I couldn't ask for Anne, because I couldn't ask it for myself. I wasn't sure I had what I needed (or that I was willing to give what was needed) to be a part of her solution. Instead, I created the opportunity to talk with her so that I could add a measure of understanding to my confused frustration regarding her situation. I stopped by the kitchen after my work hours, a time when I knew she'd most likely be alone and less busy than usual.

"Hi, Anne." I approached her while she worked at the kitchen sink. When she turned her face toward me and offered the only version of a smile she could muster, my heart fell. She was hurting, and I could feel it. It wasn't like before—the old condition driven, historically supported sadness and heaviness from the past—it was hurt. As I took her in, I experienced what I imagine it would be like to share someone's broken heart. Tears began to build in my eyes as I connected to her condition.

"Anne, are you okay?" Anne busied her hands and eyes with tasks in the sink. She freely shared details and specifics regarding one issue or another. She retold parts of her story that I'd heard before. Her relationship with her daughter still wasn't healthy. Her financial situation was still precarious. She was still trying to manage a lot of the same issues that she'd struggled with before Christ. But, in the end, I surmised this: Anne had begun her experience with Christ filled with hope but with no real clue of what that hope meant. She hoped her relationships would change. She hoped her lifestyle would change. She hoped her emotional life would change. She hoped things would get better. She hoped . . . and waited. And nothing ever changed. In response, her heart broke.

As I listened, anxiety coursed through me as if it had replaced my life's blood. I could feel myself shaking inwardly and hoped it didn't show on the outside. I rubbed my hands up and down on my pants slowly, trying to dispel some of the adrenaline that accompanied my reaction. I wasn't sure what was happening, but this encounter had definitely provoked something in me. After a while, I found it difficult to concentrate on Anne, because I was so preoccupied with trying to figure out what was happening to me.

"Well, have you talked to your pastor?" I asked the question not completely certain that it was the correct response for where we were in the conversation, but I had to speak in order to disengage from what was happening to me and re-engage in Anne's situation.

"Nnnn . . . " She barely muttered the word "no." Her face was contorted with doubt and disappointment. "Church isn't

what I thought it would be. I don't know. I guess I'm just disappointed. I thought it would be different. But I'm still saved. I just expected more."

Her final declaration was a consolation offering for me. I wanted to cry, and I was sure she could tell. I had to stop myself from sitting down right there on the kitchen floor and releasing a moan that was pushing up from my very soul. With her confession, a measure of definition came to the condition I had been struggling with for years. Anne's disappointments were mine.

I made it through our conversation, ending with a promise to pray for her and by encouraging her to keep trusting God. I made it home, completed my nightly routine, and finally placed myself in bed, ready to confront the truth that had presented itself to me during my conversation with Anne. Luckily, my husband's night owl habits gave me the space I needed for the acrobatics I feared were coming.

It started with tears. I lay quietly as a constant stream ran from my eyes onto my pillow. Then the moan I had caged away earlier found its way to freedom. I moaned until I cried aloud. Eventually, I could no longer lay. I made my way to my knees, and I confessed. I confessed my disappointment with my life as a believer. I confessed that I was unhappy and dissatisfied with my experience in the church. I confessed that I still carried

around just as much hurt and pain as I had before I'd turned to Christ. I confessed that, though I was fairly certain of my salvation, I wasn't sure of much else. I bared my heart's deepest thoughts before the Lord.

When I was empty, I was overcome with a realization. And I confessed that, too. I confessed that, even in the midst of all of this disappointment, I still had the remnants of hope stirring deep, deep within me. My final confession ushered in a relief I hadn't experienced in, what felt like, forever! As I felt liberation pouring over me like a balm, I asked the question I had been avoiding all of these years: Why? Why was I in this desolate place?

That was my moment. My willingness to acknowledge the truth of my condition began my spiritual awakening.

CHAPTER 6

AWARENESS

Ah! Now I see! / I see the what is not there / and does not have shape / but it fills up my soul / with wonder and certainty / that all is as it should be! / Now, I see.

"**D**o you love sleep?" My sister, Yvette, asked me this question one evening as we sat together enjoying the calm of after-work relaxation.

"Hmmm." I thought for a moment as I considered an answer.

Do I love sleep? I sure appreciated it. I liked that it was there for me whenever I needed it. I missed it when I could not get to it. I often daydreamed about it while pushing through the drudgery of the workday. But love? I wasn't sure.

"I do," she replied before I could decide on an answer. "I love sleep." She stared into the ceiling wistfully, as if remembering a favorite boyfriend or food. I giggled as she sighed and went on to describe her profound affection for deep, unmitigated, uninterrupted sleep.

For hours after our conversation, her question rolled around in my head. I pondered on my relationship with sleep and tried to connect with what it has meant to me over the years. It has never been easy, especially as an adult. Getting to sleep feels like a wrestling match. I toss and turn for hours, eyes squeezed shut until sleep, begrudgingly, embraces me. Even still, my victories are usually short-lived, as it is sometimes only a few hours before I awake and start the process again.

People who have a great love relationship with sleep have always baffled me. Like my husband, for instance, who can simply say, "I want to take a nap," and, within minutes be asleep. Or like my friend who slept so much that I nicknamed her Rippy, short for Rip Van Winkle. She could beckon sleep just by lying down, and she could stay asleep straight through the next day if she wanted.

The sleep experience is different for us all. Some of us are like tin soldiers when we sleep—body taut and jaw clenched so tightly that we break teeth. Others of us are like rag dolls—loose and pliable limbs, relaxed jaw and open mouth. Some of us move from end-to-end and side-to-side throughout the night, while others awake in the exact same spot where they began. Some of us even walk and talk in our sleep. Yet, there is one thing we all have in common when we are asleep: we lack awareness.

I describe awareness as possessing the ability to cognitively connect with and react to our physical surroundings through our senses. When we are aware, we can witness and respond to activity in our environment in real-time. We can fully engage in what is happening around us and are able to influence and participate. We can see the material world through our eyes and further connect with it through our hearing, touch, taste, or smell abilities. We learn, broaden our perspective, and develop higher thought processes that facilitate our mental and physical development.

Exercising awareness is physically expensive. In awareness, our various systems consume our finite resources, and this can leave us exhausted, tense, stressed, and emotional. The consuming mechanism of awareness requires a regenerative process. Hence, the primary goal of accessing sleep is restoration.

Few activities can restore us like a good night's sleep.

After a long day of toil, it is the prize. When we have exhausted our mental and physical stores for the day, our bodies crave downtime and disconnection so that we can be restored. Sleep is the socket that we plug in to, so that we can enter our next period of awareness replete.

The process that happens in the physical state of awareness also occurs in the spiritual. In both cycles, spiritually and physically, an exchange takes place that enriches and depletes us. In the physical, when we are awake, we engage in the world around us, but then we sleep and can no longer engage. Where the spirit is different, however, is that, in perfect operation, all at once, we are refilled as we expend. It can be compared to the earth's water cycle: water is drawn up out of the ocean in one place, even as it is being released into the ocean in another place. Reduction and regeneration occur simultaneously. Therefore, sleep is not a requirement in the spiritual awareness cycle. Instead, our spirits require retreat. It requires a pulling away or separation from the day-to-day activity that allows us to use our awareness solely for an intimate exchange with God.

A definition for spiritual awareness is the ability to recognize ourselves as more wholly spirit than flesh and to engage the world around us from that perspective. When we are spiritually aware, we make choices and decisions that reinforce our spiritual identity and that challenge those areas in us that do not line up with it. In perfect operation, we are consistently moving through the world in a state of complete spiritual awareness. How we show up in the world is perfectly aligned with our God-breathed identity.

Jesus' life provides us with a perfect example of what it looks like to live in full spiritual awareness. The narrative provided in the second Gospel demonstrates it best. The pace and activity that takes place in Mark is extraordinary in comparison with the other Gospels. The beginning races toward Jesus' first miracle and does not slow down afterward. There is miracle after miracle, example after example of Jesus engaging the world around Him fully from His Spirit. He heals one and then moves on to the next, and He never experiences the repercussions we have during periods of physical awareness, such as fatigue, frustration, or anxiety. Like the water cycle, we witness the absolute synchronicity of the perfected state of spiritual awareness.

One of the best examples is in chapter five. A leader in the synagogue named Jairus comes to Jesus, hoping He can heal his dying daughter. While Jesus is on His way to heal Jairus' daughter, a woman, who has a disease that causes her to constantly bleed, sneaks to the ground and touches the hem of

His garment, believing this act would heal her. Jesus stops and declares that He felt power leave Him, and the woman confesses. Jesus affirms her healing, and then he continues on to Jairus' daughter and heals her too. Healing the woman did not hinder His ability to heal the girl; for, as He gave, He received.

The example of spiritual awareness that Jesus sets for us provides an ideal lifestyle on which to pattern ourselves. His natural experience never took precedence over His spiritual understanding. He constantly moved through the world based on the truth of what He knew Himself to be spiritually. When He was challenged, when He was pressed, when He was rejected and denied, He consistently responded based on spiritual awareness, not His physical circumstance. He saw the fear in their protest, the apathy in their opposition, and the hardness of heart in their rejection. He did not allow the feedback from His flesh to shape His reaction. Instead, He responded from His spiritual awareness.

Jesus' spiritual awareness was always at its peak, and He focused on maintaining it. Throughout His life, He prioritized His connection to the father. It was as important to Him as eating or breathing. So much so that His first priority after baptism was to disconnect from the day-to-day, allowing sacred space where He could talk to and hear from God. He retreated into a quiet place, strengthened His spiritual awareness through prayer, and, in turn, received revelation for His life. Retreat became a regular part of His earthly journey.

In each of the gospels, there are several passages where we witness Jesus retreating into a quiet space to pray. Because Mark moves at such a deliberate pace, it can often be difficult to recognize the moments of retreat in Jesus' journey. However, they are there. Even with its rapid progress, Mark recounts nine times, beginning in chapter one verse thirty-five, in which Jesus enjoyed moments of retreat—either alone or with His intimate circle. At very specific moments, He would withdraw Himself away for prayer and quiet or He would pull away with His disciples to allow them space for the same.

Retreat can often feel burdensome or impossible today. Setting aside quality time in the day to intimately connect with God can feel like an intrusion on an already demanding schedule. Furthermore, when we do find time, it can feel empty and purposeless. We sit and fight with our racing minds in an attempt to make it quiet. Then we spend the rest of the time battling to keep it that way. It can be likened to the struggle some of us have falling asleep. Our tasks, our families, and the cares of tomorrow keep pulling our minds toward those thoughts, and, after a while, we give up in defeat. Our physical awareness takes priority and it seems impossible that it could be any other way.

Growing in our ability to live in spiritual awareness is difficult. In contrast to physical development, loss of awareness in the spirit does not facilitate regeneration. Instead, it induces spiritual degeneration. Sleep is necessary in our physical being. If we do not sleep, we suffer. In our spirit, however, constant awareness is the goal. If we lose awareness spiritually, we suffer. In the Bible, many passages speak to our call to always be aware. Proverbs 4 reminds us to always watch over our hearts, which is the meeting place for our will and our desire; 1 Peter 5 reminds us to be on the lookout for our enemy who prowls around in a quest to devour us; and 1 Thessalonians 5 instructs us to rejoice always and to pray without ceasing. We are called to walk in love, continue in faith, and to abide in Christ. There is no way we can achieve all of this without spiritual awareness! It is impossible. It can only be achieved through a persistent openness to the transforming, healing power of God's grace.

The challenge with spiritual awareness is that it often crashes against our physical awareness. The perfecting and shaping that takes place during spiritual development bears down on areas within us that do not align with who we are in Christ. It, unavoidably, presses against the tender areas of our souls, provoking a physical reaction through our emotions. Pressure is placed on the trauma, failures, disappointments, and hurts that we have ignored or with which we have learned to live, or even merely survive with the cloak of defeat. Then we are baited into a space where we are challenged to address them. Naturally, this process can elicit feelings of exposure, vulnerability, and fear. It can seem easier to manage the experience from a natural perspective—protect, shut down, and pretend—rather than to yield to the work that is happening in our spirit. Often, we have protected these injured areas and used them to shape our identity. We use the "That's just how I am" defense to justify where we are, never leaving room for an experience that will correct this lie. We fashion our issues into shields and walls that we hope will protect us from further injury; however, they only serve to keep us wounded and unchanged. Spiritual awareness seeks to push us out from behind our shield and to open our souls to God's healing grace. If we are going to grow in our ability to maintain spiritual awareness, we must learn to endure the discomfort it produces while trusting that God is moving us from a broken condition into healing.

On the morning that I learned of Anne's salvation experience, many years had passed since my own. I was a member of a small local church and actively engaged in its workings. I organized events, sang in the choir, and offered my support wherever it was needed. Looking in from the outside, one would have assumed that I was confident in my walk with Christ and satisfied with my life. I was not. I was desperately insecure in my relationship with Him and deeply dissatisfied with my experience as a believer. I had lost my fervor for ministry and my passion for discipleship. Many of my relationships in the church suffered from unresolved offenses, mistakes, and trespasses. I nursed a heart that had been broken by harsh words, and I was always prepared to wield my tongue as a sword. I felt rejected by leadership, even as they leaned heavily on my talents and gifts. I was alone, and my loneliness was magnified by the fact that I felt this way in the one place I did not expect to—in church.

A common experience that I have heard many believers share about their salvation experience is an overwhelming sense of redemption. You feel reset. It is as if a haze lifts from your heart, and you can see yourself and others through a clearer, kinder lens. Burdens recede, problems simplify, and people are good. You are abounding with forgiveness and love, believing the best in others and assuming they see the best in you. Your perspective is elevated, and you can see the truth above the fray. Your spirit is fully awake and, it is, in many ways, euphoric. Christ is the center of your existence, and your world finally makes sense. Yet, life keeps happening.

Life is relentless. The unchecked, nonstop momentum of our days move forward without regard for our preparedness or ability to handle what may come. It just keeps pushing usforward. We bump into others and into ourselves as life drags us through our seasons and time. It never pauses to assess our comfort or to gauge our awareness, and we are challenged to just keep moving with it at its pace. When my mother passed away, my niece made a statement that perfectly encapsulates life's relentlessness. "It feels like a holiday," she said. She wanted to know why the stores were opened and why people were still moving about as if a tragedy had not occurred. Why, we all wondered, was life continuing unchecked? But that is the nature of life. It does not allow space for us to adjust or compose. It keeps moving us forward. Relentlessly.

We are programmed by society to believe that we must keep up with life's pace in order to have value or to prove that we are thriving. We attempt to do this by leaning into our physical awareness—by rising early, working tirelessly, and fixing our thoughts on the future. We rarely pause, settle into the present moment. We permit very little time for retreat. Our internal condition becomes secondary to what we look like physically. We use material goods—a house, a car, a career, a spouse—to paint a picture that will convince our fellow travelers that we are besting life's pace. Nonetheless, if we are to live a Christ-centered life, we can no longer continue to prioritize the natural pace. Christ challenges us to focus on the condition of our soul, even as it causes us to lose our natural momentum. He insists that our identities are forged from the inside out, where the condition of our spirits are prioritized.

My transition from a redemptive demeanor into a state of discontent was imperceptible. It was the culmination of a thousand moments where I chose the physical over the spiritual. Each time that I was presented with an opportunity to lean into the spirit instead of my flesh, I took the easy, familiar option. I refused to endure the discomfort that came with confronting my spiritual distress. When I felt the pressure, I ignored it or reimagined it. I pretended to be okay when I wasn't and to care when I didn't. I avoided the people that provoked me and placed unfair expectations on those I trusted. I operated this way for years. At some point, without ever really noticing, I shut down. I still showed up, and I still participated. However, I was -

operating from a place of obligation and automation, completely disconnected and going through the motions. I was physically there. Spiritually, however, I had fallen asleep.

Getting up from my knees after my awakening, I was raw, opened wide. I felt buried and resurrected in the same space. Possibility bubbled in my soul and fear stalked it. I knew I was awake for the first time in years—since the days right after I surrendered to Christ—and I knew that this time was critical. Though I had awakened, sleep still beckoned. I had to choose to stay awake, but the idea of choosing to endure this soul-baring vulnerability was terrifying. I knew I could not make it on my own. I needed help. For the first time since giving my life to Christ, I knew that I could not live fully in Him until I gave up my natural pace and learned to completely trust Him with my spirit.

CHAPTER 7

PIECES

Does flight ever become second nature to the eagle? / Does he ride the wind mindlessly / heedless of the miracle between his soul and the ground? / Or does each time bring a speeding heart / eyelids crushed together as he falls from the cliff / wrapped in the hope that the wind will lift him / though it could choose to stay still?

I love puzzles. Whether they are literal or figurative, I enjoy the process of sifting through bits of information to determine how it all connects. I spend hours studying the shapes, edges, and shading of the various pieces as I attempt to discern how it all fits together. The satisfaction I feel when I finally figure it out is at the top of my list of favorite feelings. I feel smart, in control, and empowered. My belief in my ability to confront and subdue whatever comes next is solidified, and I am carried forward in that confidence.

At the top of my list of most undesirable emotions, however, is the feeling I have when I can't puzzle it out. There is no frustration like searching through piece after piece, arranging them by shape and color, then by shading, only to have spaces in the end where none of the pieces seem to fit. Or like believing you've found the next right piece only to discover it is not a match. It is maddening to know you have looked at the piece you need again and again without ever recognizing how and where it fits.

I once had a multi-thousand-piece puzzle that I spent hours putting together. I was meticulous in the way I sifted through the pieces. I studied the completed image, paying close attention to the subtle changes in color and shape, making sure I had a clear idea of my end goal. I then pieced together a single corner and built the image from there. If I could not find a certain piece, I would move my focus to a different area with the intention of returning to the empty space later.

When the image was almost complete, I noticed that there were a few pieces that I could not figure out. Three pieces remained; three spaces remained, but the remaining pieces did not fit the remaining spaces. I turned the leftover pieces around and around in my hand and placed them in the spaces over and over again. Yet, no matter how I positioned them, the pieces left did not fit the remaining spaces. They didn't fit, and I was beside myself. I had three pieces; there were three holes. How could none of these pieces fit in the remaining holes? For weeks, I was disturbed by my inability to complete this puzzle. It robbed me of sleep. I would lay awake longer than I wanted as I tried to unravel the mystery nightly, and I would wake up still agitated by it the next morning. It preoccupied my days. I reviewed the sample image repeatedly, studying it closely as I tried to figure out where I'd gone wrong. I brooded over the inexplicability of how the remaining pieces did not fit into the remaining spaces. I even counted the pieces to make sure I had them all, even though three remaining pieces and three remaining holes answered that question. I was at a loss, and I felt defeated. I eventually gave up, but I left the partially completed puzzle intact.

Looking back, I am amazed by how a puzzle—a simple game that was meant to be entertaining and relaxing—affected my disposition. My whole mood was shifted by my inability to successfully complete this one game. Dissatisfaction overtook me. On a small but real scale, I felt like a failure. There was a small break in the integrity of my confidence that made me question myself a little more than usual. This insignificant pastime sent a small quake through my self-esteem that provoked me to question who I believed myself to be. The fragility of our human condition is real. The blocks we assemble as we attempt to build our personal image are often held together by insubstantial materials. How caretakers defined us as children, what our friends and family believed about us as young adults, and what others say about us when we are mature adults becomes the weak adhesive that we spread between the layers of our selfhood. It does not take much for us to be pushed into a space where we are questioning foundational truths about who we are. Something as small as the inability to complete a puzzle can create a pebble of failure and send it ricocheting through our souls, leaving nicks and scrapes in the amateur masonry of our identity. You can imagine how the stones and boulders of serious life circumstances could rip holes through who we believe ourselves to be.

Our search for who we are can be likened to putting together a complicated puzzle. From the day we are born, every experience we have creates uniquely shaped life-pieces that become a part of our grand picture. Ideally, the corners of our lives are organically assembled by our childhood experience. We are cared for with love and compassion, all of our needs are timely met, and we have the security of knowing how important we are to those who watch over us. In this environment, our minds and spirits are nourished so that we have the tools we need to add the next pieces to our picture. In reality, however, many of us have childhood experiences that leave us with holes in our image. We have empty spaces in our souls, and we struggle to understand this emptiness throughout our lives. In our attempt to satisfy or fill this hollowness, we try on personalities, attitudes, relationships, and careers, exhausting ourselves with our inability to force them into spaces where they do not belong. The sheer stress from this process can be debilitating. It is often the reason why many of us—even those of us who are committed to Christ and His Church—find ourselves spiritually asleep.

The difficulty with living in awareness is learning to manage the starkness of clarity that is gained. Being spiritually asleep provides us with a warped comfort zone—a circular path of avoidance and ignorance that keeps us content and complacent. Our senses become dulled to certain aspects of our person and environment so that we deftly overlook situations that are obvious to others. We acclimate to the dark. We adjust to and normalize an existence that is steered by anxieties and insecurities. Awareness floods our internal world with light, allowing us to see clearly the truth in us and around us. We see where our issues have been inappropriately stuffed into the places where our puzzle is missing pieces. Furthermore, we struggle with the urge to keep those issues there for fear of what would come should we attempt to remove them.

I have drawers in my kitchen filled to capacity with useless, miscellaneous items. Random cords, lip balm, sewing kits, scissors, highlighters, dried ink pens, faded receipts, illegible notes, old bills, dehydrated glue stick, poultry thermometer, old phones, old eyeglasses, bandage, coins, uncapped markers, a hodge-podge of condiment packets. These items are the scraps and debris of daily life, haphazardly stored in my personal space, kept without purpose. I am sure that when I first decided to keep these items instead of tossing them into the trash that I thought I would someday need them. And, actually, I do, every now and then, slosh through these drawers in search of a random object for which I have a sudden need. Ninety-eight percent of the time, however, I do not find what I need, and, when I do, it is broken or defective. On the occasions when I conduct my unsuccessful searches, I am filled with frustrated inspiration that fuels a desire to clean up the mess. I start by randomly throwing away some of the items, but I never get far. It is not long before the pressure of having to make the decision to keep or dispose of one thing or another overwhelms me. I worry that I will throw something away that I might one day need or relocate something that I will not be able to find later. Ultimately, I shut the still messy drawer and walk away.

The process of dealing with our internal chaos can be overwhelming and, frankly, painful. Facing, often for the first time, the emotional and spiritual chaos and clutter that has been allowed to accumulate can leave us stunned, shaken, and discouraged. We wonder how it is possible that we never noticed the extent of the messiness around us. Furthermore, we have very little confidence in our ability to clean it up. The light of awareness, while necessary, is bright and revealing. Its bold presence illuminates what we have avoided and challenges us to acknowledge the missing pieces.

For months, the light of awareness uncomfortably flooded my soul. You know that feeling you get right after your senses are unexpectedly overwhelmed? Like, when you get off of a loopy rollercoaster; or when someone sneaks up behind you and yells in your ear to scare you; or the moment after you've been startled by the unexpected feeling of a small critter crawling on your arm or up your leg? That is the feeling I had for days after my awakening. I felt shaken, insecure, and out of control. Without the light, I was able to avoid seeing and feeling the reality of my condition. Darkness allowed me to thrust my traumas into obscure places in my heart and to refuse to address them. It permitted me to recline into my hurts, fears, and faults by reimagining them as enemies, dangers, and disasters. The light of awareness exposes these counterfeit conditions and allows us to see reality. Without effort, we see the nooks and crannies of our heart where we have hidden our brokenness.

The depth of vulnerability I experienced in the light of awareness was unprecedented for me, and my soul screamed for me to run back to what was comfortable. Past pain and current problems—the perpetrators of the missing pieces of my puzzle—were lit up and visible in a way they had never been before. I recognized hurts I had denied, thoughts I had nurtured, and habits I had carried that I would have sworn were not mine before choosing to live in the light of awareness. One that stood out the most was my habit of walking with my head down.

"Lift your head, girl!"

I would be walking down a random hall in a space that I cannot remember, when someone approaching from the opposite direction would say this or something like it to me. Actually, it had happened many times throughout my life: random people encouraging me to lift my head. The last time it happened was when I was learning to choose to live in awareness.

"Look up," they declared, and it hit me in my heart.

I rarely looked up. I walked with my chin dipped and my eyes cast to the floor. To be fair, being that I am an introvert, sometimes I am lost in the maze of my interior life. Often, however, though I may be in thought, it was not so deeply that it required a bowed head. This was not the by-product of subconscious activity; this was how I chose to encounter the world, with my eyes cast down. Yet, I never noticed it before. All my years, it never fully registered with me that I moved through my life with my eyes on the floor, but this time it did. And it was jarring.

Another revelation was my inability to be on time. It was the primary issue that had driven me toward awareness— Janine's attempt to help me get to work on time. I was always late, and I was confused as to why. It wasn't as if my schedule was so over-packed that timely arrival to events and obligation was impossible. I had to admit, with utter disappointment in myself, that I was late all the time because I chose to be. I would make choices that almost always assured I would not be on time, and I would convince myself that it could not have been any other way. Still, if I wanted to, if timeliness was important to me—as I had always told myself it was—I would take the necessary steps to make sure I was on time. Being late was a choice I made, and I could no longer deny it.

The revelations also showed up in the more intimate areas of my life. I realized I had overcompensated for feelings of inadequacy with an insensitive attitude. I was aggressive and opinionated, dismissive and harsh, all in an effort to cover the long-held belief that I was not enough. I recognized how insecurity drove me through most of my interactions in my life. My fear of rejection showed up in a chilly disposition and a tough exterior that ensured my vulnerable heart would not risk being unwanted. I saw the missing pieces in my puzzle that were created by my childhood where bad relationships, unhealthy eating habits, and an isolated lifestyle had been used as a substitute. I saw it all, and I had no idea what I was supposed to do. And, in this space, grace is revealed.

Grace is defined in several different ways. It is the prayer we say before we eat. It is a synonym for elegance, describing refined movement. It is the act of honoring someone with your presence. It is the state of being considerate or thoughtful. One of my favorite definitions comes from Cathleen Falsani, who gives the most basic description of grace in her book *Sin Boldly: A Field Guide for Grace* (2008). She says, "Justice is getting what you deserve, mercy is not getting what you deserve, and Grace is getting what you absolutely don't deserve." Such a simple explanation for a concept for which words are not enough. It perfectly parallels the definition of grace that most believers embrace: the unmerited favor of God.

Recognizing God's grace in our lives is commonly achieved in hindsight. There are no early notices that show up when you are about to experience grace. No signage points you in the direction of grace. No tinkling chimes or ringing bells alert you when you are in the middle of a grace-filled moment. Usually, it is only when looking back from the end of an episode that we are able truly to see grace fully. It is most often and most likely noticed when, while we are reminiscing over our prior concerns, we are awestruck by the miracle of our here and now. Yet, the beauty of grace is not found in the common but in the uncommon. The full breadth and depth of grace can only be experienced in the midst of our journey, not at its end. It cascades over us as we struggle, baptizing us with wonder. Unexpectedly, we feel grace showering down on us and, in response, are overcome by her kindness and generosity and humbled by her mercy.

Standing before my life-puzzle with all of the missing pieces and without the ability to deal with it, might have taken me under. But for the grace of God! God's grace is one of the most wonderful gifts that the believer is given. For me, His grace has been second only to His love. It is ever flowing, ever giving, and sufficient for all things. It is justice consumed by mercy and mercy expanded beyond its ends. It is the bridge that transports us from our limited existence into the eternal, inexhaustible, immeasurableness of God. God's grace is beautifully, amazingly subtle and grand all at once. With a single shift in thought, it can break you wide open and begin to minister to your pain so skillfully that you believe, impossibly, you can be better.

After months of ignoring my unfinished puzzle, I returned to it. This time, however, instead of focusing on what was missing, I took in the beauty of the image as it was. It was lovely: a picturesque thatched roof cottage sitting in the middle of a field of tall grass and wild flowers. The colors blended softly as to almost have a gauzy appearance. I took it in, allowing my eyes to appreciate the skill of the artist with gratitude for my ability to put all of the thousands of pieces together so that I could savor the beauty of the picture. After enjoying the picture for several moments, I noticed a few small gaps between some of the pieces. They didn't quite fit. And there was grace! I had simply placed the wrong parts in the wrong place, and I could only see those mistakes when I could appreciate what was in the right place. It all seemed so obvious to me then. I replaced the wrong pieces with the right ones and, finally, completed my puzzle.

The gift of grace is always available to us, most especially when we are grappling with the missing pieces of our life puzzle and do not know what to do. It is what we find when we learn to stand still and choose the light in the midst of our most difficult moments, knowing the powerlessness of darkness against a pinpoint of light. Grace gives us the confidence we need to see our missing pieces and still believe in our ability to confront and subdue whatever comes next. Grace is the wonder that sees us just as we are and whispers, "It is finished."

GIRLFRIENDS

CHAPTER 8

GEOGRAPHY

They always start in small places, those big things. / In shallow ground with too much shade / or in forgotten fields, unprotected from the heat of the sun. / They always start there. / But, now, they are big things.

Audrey Brown. For years, she and her family occupied the house on the corner of Beckett Street and Garden Avenue. It stood three houses and one field away from my family's home on Beckett and represented everything stylish and good about growing up in the seventies. Her mom, Mrs. Deenie, exuded confidence and beauty. She wore a big, beautiful afro atop her head like a queen's crown and a smile that made you feel like you belonged to her. Audrey's dad, Mr. Melvin, was cool personified, a gifted dancer whose presence filled any room he entered. Audrey and her two sisters, Denise and Cheryl, were also dancers. They were creative and bold in their self-expression and were unusually poised for teenaged girls.

Audrey was my friend. As little girls, her house was my go-to destination for play and companionship. Her family became as familiar to me as my own. Many of the memories I have of childhood center around the corner where she lived and the concrete half-wall that acted as a balance beam, a stage, and a leisure chair where we would rest and discuss the important issues of eight-year-old girls. More than forty years later, Audrey is still my point of reference for everything that was satisfying and happy about my school years. With her, I could be myself. I wasn't afraid to show the awkward uncertainty that largely defined who I was at that age. I learned to laugh with abandon—she was very funny and knew how to find the humor and joy in the most mundane and obscure moments. Her friendship made me brave. I dared to believe I was likeable, interesting, and important because she treated me that way. She taught me how to take down the wall of insecurity that surrounded me and most teenage girls, making it impossible for us to see our beauty and value.

Growing up female is tough. It is filled with ancient land mines from which few of us avoid injury. The changes that take place in a woman's being, especially during the teen years, are messy. They hurtle you into a topsy-turvy existence where aspiration, reality, physicality, and emotion are constantly crashing into each other. You are split into many by a single moment that produces competing responses. Happiness and dissatisfaction, self-admiration and self-loathing, hope and despair all battle for your mind's real estate, and you intermittently attempt to give in to all of them and none of them simultaneously.

This time in a girl's life is steeped in the sacred. Ageless lessons are handed down from the women around us, through word and deed, and we begin the arduous process of tentatively placing our feet in their various footprints to see what fits and what does not. This stage of development is also infused with harshness. We start to notice and magnify our imperfections, and fear crawls around just below the surface of our being, anticipating the moment that someone else notices them too. And someone always does. It is inevitable. The mean-girl, the betrayer, and the deceiver are inexorably a part of this experience. They put all of their energy into finding and exploiting the weaknesses of others in hopes that theirs will not be seen. To make it all even more complicated, in our hapless quest to survive, we may even find ourselves unintentionally playing these unkind roles. Yet, good friends are the remedy. They help us sort through the chaos and to quiet the noise. They sharpen our character and help us to see and choose our better selves. They teach us to recognize when judgment and unkindness are being used by us and by others to avoid our own feelings of inadequacy, jealousy, and vulnerability.

When Audrey went away to college, I visited her at the campus. While she chose college, I chose to enlist in the U.S. Air Force. I was home visiting, and reconnecting with her was at the top of my agenda. I was so excited to see my friend. As I prepared for my trip to visit her, I packed a new, form-fitting, denim dress with a cut-out back and several layers of large ruffles at the bottom. It was an unusual choice for me, as it exposed everything about my body that I had usually worked hard to hide. I hugged the pooch I carried since my hernia surgery as a child. My overly ample bosom, which made me feel disproportionate and matronly, were on display. And the cut-out back on the dress provided confirmation of just how hefty my breasts were by displaying my multi-hook bra strap. Still, I loved how I felt in that dress—sexy, feminine, and powerful.

One day during my visit, I put the dress on to get Audrey's opinion, and that was all I needed to convince me to wear it that day. I stood in the dress listening to my friend tell me how gorgeous I looked. She was so enthusiastic with her opinion that her roommates echoed her, and I believed them. Audrey left for class, and, buoyed in confidence by her admiration, I decided to take my dress for a walk around campus. I strolled through the courtyard confidently, enjoying the extended glances and appreciative comments from the guys. I reveled in the deep feeling of satisfaction that came with their admiration. On my way back to Audrey's room, I approached a corner where a young woman and man stood waiting to cross the street. I smiled broadly at them both, but my smile faded as I noticed the unkind smirk on the girl's face.

"Really?" she said to her companion loud enough for me to hear. "Why would she think that was cute?"

"I don't know," the guy replied in a tone that was laced with amused confusion, and they both started giggling.

I was dizzy with embarrassment. I fastened my eyes to the ground, waiting impatiently for the crossing signal to change. When it did, I practically sprinted across the street, and I did not look up again until I was standing in Audrey's room. When she returned from class, I told her what had happened. She proceeded to convincingly declare that the girl was jealous and that the guy was just trying to make her feel better. She told me, again, how beautiful I was in the dress and how some girls feel threatened when another woman gets attention. After a while of being coaxed and reassured, the sting from their words lost its potency, and I felt better. Although I cannot remember ever wearing that dress again, Audrey's support encouraged me to hold onto the better opinion of myself, regardless of what else may be said. She taught me to recognize the tendency some women had of using mean-spiritedness as a hiding place for low self-esteem. They place barbed wire in front of their feelings of inadequacy and fear so that no one can get close enough to see the truth of their spiritual struggle.

The propensity to engage the world from our brokenness is common—especially among women. We have all experienced the uncomfortable moment of walking into a room full of women we do not know. The head to toe inspection. The closed mouth smiles. The suspicious energy that consumes the oxygen in a room. I am sure that these types of encounters are familiar to most, if not all, of us. If not from a personal perspective, then from the countless times that this scenario has played out in movies and books. The main character of a story walks into an event solo and is immediately assaulted by eyes crawling over her in judgment and disapproval. She shifts her stance uncomfortably, and you know—without her saying a word—

that she feels unsafe and unwanted. We immediately sympathize with her, because we can easily harken back to our own version of this scene. How sweet the relief of seeing our heroine rescued by a friend!

There is something healing about being in the presence of a true friend. It has the ability to lift us above present trauma and to instantly remove the potency of our pain and discomfort. It insulates us from further injury and empowers us to be true to the highest idea of ourselves. A true friend protects us without denying our strength, leads us while walking beside us, and hears what our heart is saying—even when the words we use are contrary. They are a direct reflection of God's light and love for us, giving us permission to see and embrace the truth of who we are while allowing for our capacity to be different.

As I write this, I am overcome with gratitude for Audrey. So much in that single story about the dress displays how her friendship was a representation of God's grace and love for me. And this story is just one of many. She provided me with a refuge as a young girl. With her, I could share my deepest hurts and embarrassments openly, never worrying that I would be betrayed or rejected or pitied. She helped me to see the best side of every situation and the best in myself. She convinced me that I was a champion who was destined for greatness, and that I deserved to be loved. Her friendship set a bar of expectation for me regarding what a friend should be and gave me the security I needed to risk opening my heart to the potential for deep, abiding bonds with other women.

The friendships we develop as young girls have an immense impact on how we see ourselves and how we see other women in our adulthood. They moor us to the foundation of our history, reminding us that, no matter how far we go, we have a home to which we can return. These friendships allow us to practice sharing who we are long before we are even one hundred percent sure of ourselves. Like a baby in a childproofed space, they give us permission to explore the depth and breadth of our burgeoning identity without consideration for the presence of potential danger. Their devotion teaches us self-acceptance. Their critique encourages introspection. Their laughter shows us how to access personal joy. Their acceptance and companionship affirm our value.

One of the things I miss most about being a child is the ease with which I could make a girlfriend connection. For instance, I cannot remember how many of my childhood friendships began. They probably started under the most mundane of circumstances, so much so that they seem as if they just always were. More than likely, these bonds materialized in the time between seconds from the essence of simple interactions. They blossomed while we were standing next to one another in the lunch line or during a game of tag. They spark to life during a mutual laugh or shared treat. These friendships, that carry us through our school years and, sometimes, transition with us into adulthood, are not birthed from grand gestures and important occasions. They are the by-product of moments so tiny that they rarely leave an imprint on our memory. But the foundation of security and belonging that they solidify in us becomes a permanent part of our story.

I am sometimes grieved for today's youth. My daughter's generation, those born in the 90s and later, are growing up in very different circumstances. Childhood seems to have lost some of its enchantment. Youthful bonds are no longer easily or organically formed. Kids are now handcuffed together through manufactured moments that start and end at the whim and convenience of their parents. They no longer play outside all day discovering the joys and wonders of life together until the streetlights come on. Nor do they breezily wander from one edge of the neighborhood to the other in a quest to transform a few square blocks into a realm filled with hidden treasures and exciting adventures. Electronic devices now fill the space between those seconds that hold the bloom of connection. The vibrant colors of play have been pixelated, and the dimensions of exploration have been flattened. The perpetuation of allergies, safety concerns, and social phobias make an act as simple as sharing a treat risky. Growing up has warped into a formal affair full of scheduled activities that exhaust and subdue children rather than inspire them. Though they may thrive in other areas, the art of building solid friendships is not one of them. And I wonder what the implications of this are for the development of their souls.

It took me decades to fully embrace and integrate the lessons that I learned from my childhood friendships, especially those I garnered from my connection to Audrey. For many years, I struggled with low self-esteem. I questioned my value as a person and was doubtful of my ability to live up to what was expected of me as a woman. I looked to be reassured about my choices and actions by individuals who were not yet clear about their own. I expected men whose character contained serious deficits to cover and console my fragile heart and ego. I accepted lies as truth and traded my integrity for short-lived, shallow thrills. Yet, through all of it, I never completely lost my way. I never floated away into catastrophic territory from which I could not return. The friendships I developed as a young girl tethered me to a foundation that was substantial enough to bear the strain and pressure endured during the difficult season of my life.

I am no longer close to many of the girlfriends with whom I grew up. Including Audrey. We often pass by one another on social media. A picture is liked, a moment is shared, or a comment is made. But the depth of familiarity and comfort we once shared has faded into nostalgia. This is not by design. I am sure that she, like me, believed the closeness we once shared would endure throughout our lives. *It is too wonderful*, we believed, *too meaningful and solid. Surely our children will play together on a new corner, creating their own divine foundation and bond of friendship.* We did not account for geography. Physical distance, squired by time, untied our bond, leaving only the memory for us to cherish. Still, we both remain tethered to our foundation. This foundation that gave and still gives us a platform on which to stand as we reach up toward our hearts' desires. It stabilizes us when our world is tilted and shaken by grief and disappointment. It elevates us above our mistakes, enabling us to see beyond them. It is engraved with the lessons from our history, a cannon of wisdom that we can pass on to our children. It remains a touchstone, a place of honor for us—for our friendship—that will stand as a beacon of goodness and light throughout the rest of our lives.

CHAPTER 9

MOUNTAINS

What I long for most is my unfurling / to spread wide before the window of creation / covered only by / my words, my deeds / without explanation or apology / and to be loved anyway.

W omanhood is complex. The whole of the feminine cannot be reduced to simple terms. Unique outer traits joined with elaborate biological functions are enough to categorize women as complicated. We were fashioned in exquisite detail, endowed with delicate systems, and mingled with sharp instincts, graceful endurance, and relentless determination. We are power and tenderness, guide and novice, encouragement and boundaries in a single form. We have an inimitable role in creation that can only be described as an expression of divine love.

For men, endeavoring to understand women can be challenging and can often feel impossible. Men, who are groomed to define their experiences in terms of black and white, find themselves at a loss when trying to maneuver the bright, colorful world of the feminine. They are challenged with assimilating to the nuanced shifts of our moods and thoughts. They are baffled by the mysterious ways in which passion flickers to life or suddenly dies within us. And they must learn to ascertain what we are really saying when we speak, because it often differs from what they hear. We ask for intimacy and demand our space. We have specific needs but chafe at the idea of having to speak those needs out loud. We are clarity and conflict, tears in joy, and laughter through fear. We are not simple arithmetic. We are geometry.

I have been married for over twenty years. My husband has seen me through my daughter's toddler and teen years, as well as through her transition into independence. He held me as I descended into uncertainty after my mother died. He has watched as I nurtured the sprout and promise of new friendships and comforted me when I mourned the withering away of unhealthy ones. He has listened as I spoke from the depths of my heart with conviction and stayed silent when I contradicted that heart the very next day. He has witnessed and forgiven the darkest sides of my behavior, but he repeatedly identifies me according to my light. He is my best friend, because he is intentionally constant and consistent in my life. Yet, I am compelled regularly to drag him into emotional conversations about how little I believe he knows me. Although I am sure that he loves me and appreciates my many gifts and attributes, I long for him to seek to discover more of me.

I recently read this wonderful story by comedian and writer Sara Benincasa on the online publishing platform "Medium." It begins with a succinct analogy of what we, in our humanness, see when we encounter one another. She wrote,

When we look at a mountain we see one face of it, and even if we wake up and gaze at that same mountain every single morning of our lives, we do not see its wholeness. We can hike it, fly over it, traverse its circumference a thousand times and still we won't see its entirety, every layer, every element, every atom. To know a mountain, or a person, is to see a whole being in its fullness at all times in all seasons—every mood, every moment. If there is a God, this is what God sees. But we are not gods, and so our view, no matter how vast, is always partial.

This description reverberates through me like the ringing of a struck gong. She wrote it in response to the suicide of a well-known TV personality who appeared to have lived a life of joy, privilege, and adventure. He traveled the world, met important and interesting people, and did amazing things. Yet, he took his own life. It was shocking, to say the least, for someone who seemed to have such an abundantly satisfying existence to take his own life. It jarred those who believed they knew him as much as it did those who watched him from afar. It magnified what is true about the substance of many relationships: those who believe they know the mountain are, really, only familiar with its face.

I love maps. Having the ability to trace the various pathways from town to town, city to city, and state to state fascinates me. Before cell phones and GPS systems, I would purchase the large road atlas from the bookstore and examine the various courses that lead from one place to another in different parts of the country. Whenever my husband, Michael, and I would take a trip, I would always pressure him to exit the highway and drive the lesser-known roads through the countryside and small towns that form the beauty and character of our country. Once, we drove through the mountains on a return trip after visiting family in North Carolina. On the way there, our agenda left no time for us to forgo the speed and convenience of the highway. On the way back, however, we were free to take our time. I pulled out a map and found a route that led us home by way of obscure mountain byways. After some convincing, Michael veered right to exit the highway into the hills, and we proceeded to wind upward and to move deeper into the mountain on a two-lane road.

As we drove, we slowed our pace as much as possible and took in our surroundings. The landscape was a mixture of harshness and beauty. The craggy stone of the hillsides was softened by wild, lush greenery that fringed the edges and peeked through the heart of the rock sporadically. There were waterfalls tucked back into small coves, trees decorated with large colorful blossoms, and artistic patterns weathered into the hard surfaces by the elements and time. Without the pressure of traffic tailing close behind, we were able to savor the sights. We pointed and oh-ed and ah-ed our way through the scenery until we were slowed to a full stop by a line of traffic. Every few moments, the traffic would move forward for some seconds before abruptly stopping again. We inched along the path, wondering what was happening ahead to cause the delay. After creeping along for a while, old buildings started to appear on either side of the road. Houses and businesses that resembled the architecture in photos of Western towns from a by-gone era overtook the natural scenery. We entered a quaint little town, comprised of mostly wooden structures, tall and narrow, some painted in neutral tones, others sporting bare wood. The sound of music began to waft through the air, and decorated booths advertising crafts, food, and other wares were stationed along the road's edge in front of the buildings. People milled along the streets, leisurely stopping to peruse or purchase the goods. We took in the lively activity, feeling as if we had been granted access to an intimate, hidden part of the mountain. There was so much life in this obscure place! Had we never ventured beyond the face of the mountain, we would have missed it.

Mountains, on their face and from afar, are beautiful. They are majestic and awe inspiring in their position in the vista. They provide our imagination and our aspirations space to stretch and reach. The base of a mountain seems unshakable, and its peak communes with the clouds. They are a dwelling place for mythological gods and a virtual home for our souls. We are grateful for the views they provide us from our distant decks and balconies, for the slopes they offer us when we open ourselves to adventure, and for the confidence they bolster in us when used in analogy. We are in love with the features and lines of a mountain, the massive weight and substance of its exterior, but rarely do we desire to venture beyond its face so that we can know its heart.

Mountains are intimidating, and venturing into the bosom of one can be frightening. While they are shelter for small, furry creatures that make our hearts swell with mirth, we could just as easily encounter large, fierce creatures that would paralyze the body with fear. There are fragrant flowers and poisonous weeds, plain rocks and priceless stones. There are caverns that can consume us with their darkness and coves that can enlighten us with their charm. Mountains are so menacing and complex that they can seem dangerous to navigate and impossible to know. So, there is comfort in traveling the roads that take us around the mountain or through the well-worn paths that have been tried and proven safe. We still get to enjoy it as spectacle, but we never have to confront the parts of it with which we are unfamiliar or need to figure out the pieces that we do not understand.

As women, we are encouraged to hide the complexity of who we are far behind the face of our mountain—to conceal the roughed-up ground and unhewn landscape that represents the trial and error of our efforts to be better. The world raises us to fear that we may one day be exposed for who we are: imperfect, unfinished, repeatedly altered beings with a history that is shaded by darkness and light. There are scars; though we survived our trouble, we were not unscathed. There are tear-laden junctures that record how and where we were undone. We are told that, if we show these parts of us, we risk being labeled as unworthy or as failure. So, we work to present ourselves—our surface—as polished, complete, impervious, and whole. We shelter our substance behind an image that we cultivate to fit the social narrative created for us, but not by us. We smile, we laugh, and we discuss the news and weather. We always answer with "great" or "fine" when asked about our well-being (because we should not answer otherwise). And, to those who only want to see the mountain's face, we are sound and all is well. Even still, we all long for the brave soul who is willing to venture the tall grass and the stony path that will take him, or her, behind the mountain's face.

One of the great struggles of relationship is how we all desire to be intimately known and deeply loved; yet, we hold sacred and fiercely protect the details that open a pathway toward a deeper understanding of who we are. We tuck them away in the dark corners of our memory; we cut them down to fit the narrow spaces that we allow for our social narrative; or we keep them so high above our present day that the specifics are impossible to see. This fear-based tendency poses a perplexing equation with obscure factors and hidden variables that make it challenging for those who may want to know us more. It is geometry, and it must be deciphered before one is able to venture beyond the face of the mountain. Still, even as we guard the path that leads to the heart of who we are, our souls yearn to be seen and known. We crave companionship in those dark, narrow, and high places. We want to share the memories and monuments from our journey and, in return, hear a friend say to us, "You are, still, okay."

I have made so many female friends in the course of living—people I have met through classes or travel or work— with whom I have lost touch. Beautiful souls with lovely faces who have impressed me with their presence and showed an interest in my mountain's face. I have shared simple life details, laughs, and light lamentations with them in the common spaces that birthed our connection—the office, the classroom, the public square—and I have parted from them with very little care for whether we would meet again. I made sure to keep any pain or problems I may have fully concealed behind the forest of my wit and wisdom and to maintain a pleasant appearance. I never shared the intimate or the most interesting bits of my life with them, and I never searched behind their smiles or between their words for clues as to how I could know them better. Yet, in the midst of our conversations, I would make comments like, "well, you know me" or "yeah, I know you," while understanding that they did not truly know me and I did not truly know them. Every now and then, however, a cursory acquaintance would transform into a good girlfriend and I am blessed.

The people in our lives who choose to take the expeditious routes in their quest to know us, instead of the scenic by-ways, often miss the most special and interesting parts of who we are.

They never get to witness the beautiful greenery that God uses to decorate the craggy hillsides of our once broken heart. Nor will they fully understand how the blossoming trees and fragrant bushes of our personality are sustained by the waterfall of tears from our past disappointments. They will never hear the story of how God's grace slowed us down enough for us to appreciate the changes that He has wrought in our lives. And, most of all, they will never be able to comprehend our desire to celebrate our journey to this point. Those satisfied with our mountain's face fail to grasp that what they see from the outside cannot compare to the splendor that is found within. What a beautiful gift are those girlfriends who are willing to take the scenic route.

I appreciate my husband. He is irreplaceable and unmatched as my life partner. No one knows the highways and main thoroughfares of my personality like he does. In fact, parts of me are more easily accessible to others because of his willingness to do the work that created a clearing and a pathway there. Still, I have come to understand that there are places in me that he cannot know and places in him that will remain foreign to me. In these places, there is a language barrier, and, no matter how much we study one another, we will never be fluent enough to breach it. And this is okay. We cannot know everything. We can only know so much. As Benincasa said in her article, we are not gods. But there is a God, and He does not leave us hopeless and yearning. He graces us with good girlfriends. These girlfriends, who speak our language, are map connoisseurs. They know that there are routes that will take them behind the mountain's face. For, they are mountain, too; and they recognize that the true majesty of who we are is best experienced from the inside. So, they look for the off-ramp that will carry them higher and deeper into our mountain, and, when they find it, they enter reverently and offer themselves as a conduit for God's love.

Good girlfriends will risk the dark caves of our history, venture the narrow canyons of our personality, and will climb the steep cliffs of our insecurity in their quest to know us better. They will do the geometry necessary to figure out our composition and honor the path we took to be who we are. Although they will never know our mountain like God knows it—every layer, element, and atom, in all seasons, moods, and moments—they will push to know what they can. They will lean into and celebrate the peaks of our topography—the places where we shine and are confident and sure—and their belief in us will empower us to stand more boldly in our place on the landscape. They will also work to move beyond the overgrown brush, the thickets and thorns of our hurt, fear, and brokenness. They will sit beside us there and listen as we struggle to be healed. They will labor to know us there, so that they can love us in those places too.

CHAPTER 10

SISTERS

My heart / fits your hand / perfectly.

M y sisters and I are close. We genuinely enjoy being around one another. We are each other's confidantes, counselors, critics, supporters, and resources. We never laugh as much, cry as freely, or feel as accepted as we do when we are together. We are bold, loud, confident, and comfortable in one another's presence. We prefer our own company, and it is obvious to anyone else who is in relationship with us. My good girlfriend Mary, who has been one of my closest friends for over twenty-five years, once described being in the midst of the sisters as inspiring but intimidating. I would venture to guess that this is the opinion held by many of our friends. Those of us who are married are often faced with the competitive dynamic that can arise between the sisters and the spouses. Husbands feel left out, ignored, or forgotten when the sisters are together. Over the years, however, we have learned to read and deftly maneuver these situations. Much to our spouses' chagrin, this can often mean planning girls-only trips! In any event, we have stayed close and worked to nurture and grow our relationships.

As it is within any group, there are varying levels of relationship between us. Our ages span generations, and, therefore, we have differing stages of historical attachment. Our life-paths cover widely dissimilar ground, giving us wildly contrasting points of view. Our personality types cover every aspect of the spectrum from seriously introverted to unmistakably extroverted. We clash and disagree, and we experience serious conflict. Yet, even with all of this diversity and through our many trials, we stay fiercely committed to our sisterhood. We do this by staying anchored to the foundation that was established for us as children.

From our beginning, my parents insisted that my siblings and I stay tightly bonded together. My father used intimidation to keep us connected. He was a passionate protectionist who insisted on us being unconditionally loyal to one another. "That's your sister!" he would yell whenever we fought or refused to fight for each other. To drive his point home, he would end our disputes by having us stand in the middle of a room in an embrace. Those moments are still the funniest and most agonizing memories we share. We would loosely wrap our arms around one another, tears streaming down our faces as we angrily sobbed in protest. In contrast, my mother's approach was much more subtle. She worked to ensure that we prefer our sisters above anyone else. She would constantly remind us of the temporary nature of other people and of how your sisters, on the other hand, are an inextricable part of your foundation. At the same time, she taught us that, by first learning to understand and appreciate each other, we could grow our sisterhood beyond our enclave and inspire deep, life-long connections with other women.

It took many years for us to grow into the level of relationship that we have now. We had to overcome disappointment, dissension, betrayal, recklessness, and trauma along the way. There were many times when our sisterhood survived simply because we used our father's tenacity and ferociousness to cling to one another through difficult times. Yet, when the storm was over, we needed more than brute strength to move us beyond whatever threatened our commitment to one another. It took the lessons from our mother for us to get over our crisis and to be better. When the dust settled, we had to be able to embrace humility by asking for or receiving forgiveness. It required us to extend kindness by allowing our faith to override our feelings and to give grace by seeing beyond the inadequacy of our humanity. We had to practice compassion, demonstrate generosity, and live out the values of love. We also had to realize that doing any of this by ourselves was impossible. It could only be done through a relationship with Jesus and an understanding of His Word.

Mommy's relationship with God's Word was extraordinary. I have very rare recollections of her quoting scripture, but there is not one memory of her in my mind that is not representative of how she lived it. Her life demonstrated the power and peace that you could garner from God's Word. It was her anchor and her guide. She began every day in His Word. A cup of coffee, a piece of jellied toast, and an open Bible. Through trauma, heartbreak, tragedy, loss, prosperity, accomplishment, ease, celebration, and sickness: this morning ritual never changed. She relied on God's Word to settle her day before it began. "It'll keep you, if you want to be kept," she would declare about it whenever we needed a reminder. It informed every aspect of her life, including the way she showed up for her family and friends. Her living example solidified in us the need for us to build our lives—including our relationships—on the solid foundation of God's Word.

On Christ the solid rock I stand / All other ground is sinking sand. These words are from the hymn, "My Hope Is Built," written in 1834 by Edward Mote. They are my most favorite lyrics of any song I've ever heard. It encapsulates the lesson my mother worked to instill in her children. Nothing created can be sustained without its foundation being forged by the Word. It is eternal, and it is relevant in every age. It amazes me that Edward Mote was considering the stability of his ground in the 1800s in much the same way I consider mine today. His Word forces you to examine the substance of your life and to build relationships with the tools you garner from it. It will teach you to sift through the rocks, dirt, and debris that can distort how you experience those you love and do the work to build something real and meaningful. It teaches us to be spiritual geologist.

The year I turned forty, my mother died. For many years, she had dealt with various health challenges before her body finally succumbed to them. When she became ill, it was life-altering for my siblings and me. Mommy was our go-to. She always answered our calls and listened with patience. She picked up kids from school and cared for them when we were stuck at work. She saw us through hardships—financial, marital, and emotional. We were always welcomed back into her home, for her home remained ours no matter how far away we strayed. She bailed us out when it was wise and prayed for us to get the lesson when it was not. She kept us connected and helped us to recognize the good in each other. She persistently redirected our focus to Christ, and she lived a life that was a constant reminder to keep Him as the main thing in everything. In this life, she was our rock. Her illness reversed this dynamic, teaching us to be for her what she had always been to us. And, when she passed away, it shook our foundation.

Since my mother's death, my sisters and I have held a conference call every Saturday morning. We live in various parts of the country, and this allows us to stay engaged. We share stories from our weeks, give updates on what is happening in the lives of our children, and talk about our various trials. We laugh, cry, and, sometimes, sing. Then we get down to our primary purpose. We pray and study God's Word. It is our way of staying connected to the legacy our mother left for us and to reinforce the bonds she forged in us. Sometimes we use books to guide our discussion, other times we are each assigned a week where we are tasked with leading the discussion about a scripture that is meaningful to us. Whatever approach we decide to use, we stay focused on God's Word. This ritual has endured for more than ten years. It is our attempt to replicate the morning coffee, jellied toast, and Bible for ourselves. Different family members have joined the call for a short time, like our children who have not yet recognized the importance of our ritual. Others have become a permanent part of our process, like my mother's younger sister, our Aunt Marion, and our cousin Carol (whom we call Aunt Carol because she is senior to us and because she deserves to be honored as such) and her lovely daughter Lauren. We have each gone through periods where we chose to forego the call and seasons where the weekly calls were essential to our survival. Regardless of who called in and who did not, the calls continued and consistently stayed focused on God's Word.

Our commitment to prioritizing God's Word as our primary connecting point has transformed our relationships tremendously. Where we once saw our presence in each other's lives as conditionally optional, we now understand that it is eternal. We have learned to elevate our spiritual sisterhood above our natural one. The Word has forced us to become geologists. We have learned to sift through the earth and debris of our beings in order to build our relationships on solid rock.

There is a scene from my mother's home-going celebration that remains sharply rendered in my memory. It is the first image that surfaces whenever I think about that day. We were all gathered around her casket to say our final goodbyes. All in white; all silent. We clutched onto one another as we grappled with the gravity of that moment. For days leading up to her funeral, we were caught up in the endless activity and conversation regarding how we could best honor her life. Flowers, colors, obituaries, speakers, readings, songs: these details consumed our minds, temporarily allaying the weight of our grief, allowing us to feel light enough to continue with the ordinariness of life. We went to dinner, called work to address any pressing issues, and discussed ordinary, everyday lifematters all while in the midst of planning for our goodbye to her. Yet, in the moment when we stood before her for the final time, there was nothing else. The heaviness of losing her took over. The sadness of never seeing her again, the burden of her illness, the consequences of our choices, and the condition of our various relationships descended on us all at once. Insecurity coursed through my body like a parasite threatening to eat me alive. What would happen next? We were a bouquet of colorful balloons that sometimes crashed into and pushed away from one another. How would we stay together if she were not holding the strings? How would we stay "us"? Furthermore, would my siblings want to stay connected to me? I was a minefield of rocks and debris—flawed, sometimes dark and depressed, and, often, too opinionated. I imagined it would be easy for them to float away from me.

As we stood together, attempting to process her loss, as individuals and collectively, I began to tremble internally under the horrible weight of it all. I was desperate for us to stay there as a collective, feeling the same pain, suffering the same fate. After a few moments, we were joined by my Aunt Carol. Irritation shot through me when I saw what I perceived as her attempt to bring our goodbye to a close. I was not ready, and I did not want to be rushed. I wanted to stand there until I could no longer stay upright. Standing there meant it was not finished. Standing there meant our strings were all still connected, and as long as we were there, Mommy's presence would continue to hold them together.

Aunt Carol stood there, her arms wrapped around us, and we all silently communed for a few moments. Then she said, "This is the day the Lord has made; I will rejoice and be glad in it." I wanted to bristle at her words. I wanted to declare that I could not rejoice, I could not be glad, but I knew that that was not true. I knew this because of the foundation my mother had placed beneath us. I could rejoice. I could look beyond the fear and anxiety that threatened to define this experience for me and find refuge in God's Word.

As Aunt Carol quoted the Psalm, my siblings and I looked at one another. We were all wondering the same thing. "Is this okay?" We each wanted to know if the others were okay with ending our goodbye and moving forward with what was next. I was comforted a little when I recognized the same insecurity and anxiety in their faces that, I was sure, I wore on mine. Looking at them, I knew, like me, they were not ready. We were not okay. We were all afraid that, if we left from standing there, something would be irreparably broken and destroyed. Yet, we knew we could not stand there forever. We had to move forward. We had to grab ahold of what was available and persevere. So, we all took hold of the scripture.

"This is the day the Lord has made," we repeated in unison. "We will rejoice and be glad in it." Then we took our seats.

Whenever I look back at that day, my heart swells with gratitude for Aunt Carol. With grace and wisdom, she offered us the only possible remedy to our sorrow. By encouraging us to remember our foundation, she helped us find our strength. Speaking that single scripture lifted our heaviness just enough that we could see beyond the facts of the moment and into the grace and truth of its meaning. The fact is that this moment was inevitable. In a perfectly ordered world, this scenario would still be. We all die, and we will all lose the physical presence of those we believe we cannot live without. And life, unrelentingly, will go on. Yet, the truth of God's Word tells us that, though they are not present with us, they are not gone. They "only slip away to the next room" (Henry Scott-Holland, "Death Is Nothing at All," 3). Who they are and what they gave is still with us. They shifted, changed, and transformed us with their energy, their presence, and their words, and that impact remains. Our recitation did not remove the pain from that ordeal—our hearts were still broken and we were still anxious about what would come next—but it helped us to remember our foundation. It sparked a flame of remembrance that said, He will never leave or forsake us. Then, I remembered that, even though I grieve, He promises to give me peace beyond my understanding. Finally, I could declare that, though it was not okay, He promises that it is all good. And in that moment, my mother is proven right. The Word would keep me. If I wanted to be kept.

The legacy of prayer, faith in God's Word, and sisterhood that my mother left to us is what I value most in the world. The Word has been a guidepost and anchor for me whenever I have felt lost and unsure. It has the ability to speak to the height, depth, and width of the human condition like nothing else. Having the opportunity to speak my deepest, most personal concerns through prayer has provided me with the peace and strength I need to grow beyond my heaviest burdens. And my sisters are my original and forever girlfriends. They are my constant companions, and I am better because I have them. They have allowed me to experience the impact of God's grace like no other. They sift through the earth of my being with kindness and forgiveness, always working to keep me anchored to our foundation. No matter what changes I go through, they fight to stay connected to me. They are the geologists of my life, and I am grateful.

Bibliography

Norwood, Dorothy. 1994. *Somebody Prayed For Me.* CD. Malaco Records, Inc.

Falsani, Cathleen. 2008. *Sin Boldly.* Grand Rapids, Mich.: Zondervan.

Holland, Canon Henry Scott. 1994. *Death Is Nothing At All.* Souvenir Press.

Benincasa, Sara. 2018. "*When They Leave – Member Feature Stories – Medium*". Medium. https://medium.com/s/story/when-they-leave-8eb15cc2ee1f.

The Nelson Study Bible: New King James Version. E. D. Radmacher et al, eds. Nashville: Thomas Nelson, 1997.

About the Author
Written by her Sister, Sandra Morrow

Sheila Denise Townsend is a passionate minister of the Gospel of Jesus Christ who has been uniquely equipped to minister to His body. A native of Hamilton, Ohio, Sheila has been gifted by God as a prolific writer, psalmist, teacher and preacher. The ninth of eleven children born to the late Sherman J. and Barbara J. Fleetwood, Sheila learned to live her life in a way that glorified God from the example that was modeled at home. Her mother, Barbara, who was a minister of music for more than 50 years, imparted in each of her children a love and appreciation for praise and worship. At an early age, Sheila's gifts of ministry were evident, as individuals were often drawn to her spirit of compassion and the desire to see the broken healed. In 2000, Sheila said yes to the call of God, to use all that He has invested in her to build up the body of Christ. For many years now, she has lead a women's ministry, using 2nd Corinthians 5:17 as its foundational scripture, "*Therefore if any man be in Christ, he is a new creature: old things are passed away; behold, all things are become new.*" Through this ministry, she aids women on their journey of becoming new in Christ. This ministry has had a powerful impact on each person who has participated. Sheila served ten years in the United States Air Force as an Air Traffic Controller before returning to Ohio. She earned a Bachelor of Arts in English from Miami University, Ohio. She is a proud, devoted mother to her daughter, Jamyla, and currently resides in Hamilton with her husband, Michael.

Made in the USA
Lexington, KY
19 August 2018